Dick Walker's
TROUT
FISHING
ON RIVERS AND STILLWATERS

Dick Walker's
TROUT FISHING
ON RIVERS AND STILLWATERS

SWAN·HILL
PRESS

Copyright © 1997 Dick Walker
First published in the UK in 1997 by Swan Hill Press,
an imprint of Airlife Publishing Ltd

British Library Cataloguing-in-Publication Data

A catalogue record for this book
is available from the British Library

ISBN 1 85310 836 7

Typeset by Hewer Text Composition Services, Edinburgh
Printed in England by Livesey Ltd, Shrewsbury

Swan Hill Press
an imprint of Airlife Publishing Ltd
101 Longden Road, Shrewsbury, SY3 9EB, England

Contents

Preface

This book is a dedication to both the angling and the writing skills of Dick Walker. He remains the greatest angling writer of all time, providing a weekly column for *Angling Times* for more than thirty years, regular contributions to *Trout and Salmon*, *The Field*, *Angling* and various other magazines.

But it's not the quantity but the quality of his work which has stood the test of time. His untimely death in 1985 was a tragedy which robbed the angling world of a twentieth century angling genius. Dick Walker managed to combine the perfect blend of skill and enthusiasm with the analytical brain of the scientist. If he wrote about a subject, his comments were based on personal experience and case studies of fellow anglers. This book, based on fly-fishing skills, knowledge and personal experience, honed and analysed over many years, is a testament to the dedication and expertise of one of our greatest anglers.

His expertise is beyond dispute. Chalk-streams, small stillwaters, large reservoirs – all welcomed Dick as a regular visitor. And he was open-minded enough to fish a variety of styles and techniques – nymphs, lures and dry flies. His scientific background – he read engineering at Cambridge University and was involved in radar during World War II – gave us all an added bonus. His written work is a testament to both subjective experience and objective analysis, a rare combination. What follows is a series of articles, taken from various magazines, over a time span of more than 20 years before the author's death. These articles give the modern-day trout angler a blueprint for success. Tackle, tactics, fly patterns and general observations are covered, in full, with every article, in each section, based on a lifetime of experience.

The information contained between these pages is as relevant today as the day it first appeared in print. Read, enjoy and improve your catches. Nothing would have brought a broader smile of satisfaction to the great man's face than the knowledge that his writing had given enjoyment, and improved catches, to a fellow angler!

Peter Maskell

Further Note

It will have been noted that in some of the articles Richard advocated the use of half-blood knots. This was only up to the time that he devised the Grinner knot which he thought was vastly superior, and which he used thereafter.

Vycoat was used in his fly-tying, but I understand from Donald Downs that this is no longer available, and he recommends Devcon.

It has not always been possible to name the photographer of some of the pictures used, and for this we apologise.

PART ONE
General

Catching Your Trout

There have been many arguments among anglers about which kind of fishing demands most skill. We all admire the dexterity of the roach-fisher who strikes successfully at a bite that the majority of anglers would not have seen. The skilful exponent of casting with a double-handed salmon fly rod commands our respect, as does the dry-fly fisherman on the chalk stream or the man who really knows how to fish the wet fly on a rain-fed river.

Only those with experience of sensitive legering can appreciate the ability of a skilled practitioner in this art, but many would argue that it demands greater skill than any other kind of fishing. There are many ways of catching fish that some would claim surpass all others in the demand for skill that they impose.

Unless and until further experience makes me change my mind, I am inclined to think that catching trout in a lake or reservoir when they are feeding just below the surface places the greatest premium on sheer skill, because more variables are involved than in any other way of fishing.

Consider the problems with which the angler is faced when he sees a fish break the surface.

He has to decide:

> in which direction it is moving
> how fast it is going
> the depth at which it is feeding

He has to cast his fly so that it alights in the right place at the right time. Having cast it, he must decide which is the right moment at which to move it, and what form that movement should take.

The probability is that the length of line he has out, and the direction in which it lies, are both wrong when he sees the rise. He has to lift off, shorten or lengthen line and recast in a different direction, for which he has all too little time.

If more than one fish is seen to rise within casting range, the angler must decide in a split second to which one he will cast. It may be clear that the choice is between two fish of different sizes, and fate usually ordains that the smaller will be the easier.

All these difficulties may lead one to think that casting to individual fish is less likely to produce results than methodical casting and retrieving in the area where trout can be seen feeding.

That may indeed prove successful, sometimes very much so. Whether it is more successful than casting to individual fish depends very much on how good the angler is at solving quickly the time and space problems that are involved. Ability in that is born of constant practice, which is why I think it pays always to try for the individuals, because the more you try, the better at it you become and the more often you succeed.

My own practice is to spend some time in methodical casting and retrieving, while at the same time watching for rise-forms and trying to judge from them how fast the fish are moving and not only what they are eating but also the depth at which they are feeding. In the latter respect a few inches can make a lot of difference. Sometimes the trout are taking insects in the surface film, sometimes pupae rising to hatch, and this they may do only an inch or two below the surface, or at some intermediate level between that and two feet or more.

Of course, they may be feeding at a still deeper level, but then the opportunity to cast to individuals we can see is no longer present.

When taking insects in the surface film, the mouth of the trout as well as its dorsal fin and tail-tip all break the surface. When taking insects a few inches down, the dorsal and tail-tip break surface but the mouth does not. Feeding at still greater depths may be indicated by swirls or what I have come to call a 'shatter' – a movement of water resembling a tiny subsurface detonation. Feeding at still greater depths is shown by calm patches appearing in a ripple, or a barely perceptible movement, usually circular, of small items of debris in a calm surface.

All this leads the angler to decide which pattern of fly to try, and how far ahead of the estimated path of the fish to cast, in order to allow it to sink to the right level. The sinking rate of the chosen dressing has to be taken into account, but some regulation is possible by varying the rate of movement after casting: the faster you pull, the shallower the fly will fish. Of course if you pull too soon or too fast, your fly will move out of the track of the fish – unless you have cast beyond that track in the first place, which it may sometimes pay to do.

It all becomes much easier in a breeze because then most of the fish will be travelling upwind, usually all at the same pace. The pace is probably dictated by the density of the insects on which the trout are feeding; the fewer there are, the faster the fish travel. By observing disturbances, it is possible to judge their speed, though it is all too easy to assume that successive disturbances are made by the same fish when in fact more than one is responsible. It is a good idea to wait a while if in doubt about this.

In calm conditions, there is no telling which way a fish may go after

4

producing a surface disturbance. It may be possible to see which way it is pointing, and that can help, though a fish will often change direction. If possible, therefore, it is best to cast as fast as possible straight into the rise-form, but it must be done very quickly indeed, otherwise you will only cast where the fish was, not where it is. Consequently, a breeze that knocks up a nice little ripple is a great advantage; it allows the angler more time to vary both distance and direction, and to cast ahead of a fish whose movement is predictable in both direction and speed.

I find it helps, on seeing a rise-form, to look immediately at the place where I expect, on a snap judgement, the next one to appear. At the beginning of a spell of this sort of fishing, one is seldom right, but the appearance of the next rise-form elsewhere provides the basis for improved judgement, and after a time accuracy improves greatly. If then the fly is cast where the next rise is expected, the chances of its arrival coincidentally with the fish are likely to improve accordingly.

Opinions differ about this, some saying that the fly should fall as nearly as possible on the nose of the fish, others taking the view that the fly should arrive before the fish, being moved when the fish arrives. In my experience, both techniques can be successful, and it matters little which is chosen when the trout are very near the surface. When they are deeper but still causing visible disturbances, then one has to take sinking times into account, and cast ahead of the fish in time, so that the fly has sunk to the right depth when it arrives.

It remains only to add that when two anglers are fishing from a boat, teamwork is essential, otherwise lines will cross and tangle frequently. Friends who fish together often develop an excellent understanding about who shall cast to which fish, each knowing instinctively which of them has the best chance at any riser that is seen, acting accordingly and swiftly.

I think many will feel greater satisfaction at catching a fish at which they have deliberately cast than one that appeared from nowhere and took a fly fished at random.

Advice for Beginners

While most of the advice that appears in fishing magazines is thoroughly sound, it remains true that the experienced angler can fish successfully in a way that would involve the novice in all kinds of trouble. You wouldn't put a driver who had just passed his driving test into the seat of a Grand Prix Ferrari and expect him to drive like a world champion!

So here is some advice for the out-and-out novice. First, learn to cast with a light, easy-action rod, carrying a medium line, say No 6 or No 7. Let the rod be about 8 ft 9 in to 9 ft 3 in.

Just because some expert with a fist like a ham and a grip like a gorilla tells you how to cast a No 10 Hi-D line 45 yd, using a carp rod blank with a fly rod handle, you are apt to think you can handle such equipment. Well, you can't, and you'll be in dreadful trouble if you try. Stick to tackle that is easily handled in your first season. Learn to cast 25 yd in an easy style, so that you can go on doing it for hours. You catch no fish while you're sitting on the bank nursing an aching forearm and shoulder. You're not even learning anything.

When you've had a season of weekly or bi-weekly outings, your muscles will have developed enough to let you consider more powerful equipment. And when you're learning, use mainly floating lines, never fast sinkers. Sinkers need experience, especially fast ones. Make a cast with one, pause a bit too long, your fly is in the bottom. It snags, or comes up plastered with silkweed. Maybe you get a backing tangle: before you can clear it, the line's on the bottom. Maybe you forget that after retrieving a sinking line, you have to make a roll cast, not lift off as you would a floater. So you attempt a lift-off and crack the rod, or even snap it clean off just above the butt.

Don't risk it. Stick to the floater until your casting is fully under control.

Arthur Cove is a master angler, and was an expert before half the magazine readers had started school. He can handle a leader carrying three flies, 14 or 15 ft long, with no bother whatever. The novice can't. Here is a list of fun and games that a novice can become involved in by trying to fish three flies.

1. One fly in a fish and another in a boat bottom.
2. One fly in a fish and another in the net mesh.
3. Two fish on at once. You lose the bigger one.
4. One fly in a fish, one in jacket.
5. One fly in the net mesh, one in your trousers or sock.
6. Top fly in top ring, trout plunges, gets off.
7. A diabolical leader tangle involving all three flies, usually at dusk when you can't see to untangle it, and fishing stops in 15 minutes.

Long before you're as good as Arthur Cove – if you are destined ever to become that good – you can use two or three flies. But not in your first season. Stick to one fly for that time. And don't try ultra-long leaders, either. Learn to handle 9- or 10-ft leaders first, with your single fly at the end.

Three flies are not three times as likely to tempt a trout, or be seen by trout, or catch three times as many trout. In his first season, an angler will catch just as many trout with one fly, probably more, because he won't waste time with the troubles I listed earlier. You catch no trout when one fly is stuck in your hat and another is in the seat of your trousers, while the third is blowing in the wind trying to get hooked into something else.

I am not as good as Arthur Cove or Bob Church, but I seldom fail to catch a few trout when I try, and I'm not exactly a stranger to limit bags. I've done a lot of fishing with two or three flies on the leader but nowadays you seldom see me using more than one. My catches haven't decreased because of it, though I have to admit that after all these years in which I've been trout fishing, I'm more likely to have the right fly on my leader than a novice is.

Next, don't worry too much about distance casting. True, being able to throw a long line is very useful, especially on reservoirs, but being over-concerned with it, and trying too hard, will not give you the ability you want. Long casting is not the result of using extra effort. Too much effort allied to a defective style will shorten your distance, not increase it. So concentrate on a smooth, easy style. Get it all together and the distance will improve automatically.

Never try to see how far you can cast. Instead, see by how much you can reduce the effort you use and still make a nice tidy cast of 20–25 yd. Stand so that you can turn your head and watch your back-cast. You can then see if you are doing it correctly and if not, how to alter the way you do it, so as to get it right.

There's no way you can make a good forward cast without first making a good back-cast. The back-cast is the one that is hardest to learn to do properly.

Finally, don't be shy. Every angler was a novice once. There are very few experienced anglers who aren't willing to spend a little time in helping a fellow angler who is new to the game. So don't be afraid to ask for help. Perhaps once in a while you may get a surly answer, in which case you'll know you asked someone whose advice wouldn't have been worth much, even if you had received it. Only – don't ask for advice from a chap who is wading out to start casting, or who has a fish on, or is sorting out a tangle! Wait till you can claim his attention without spoiling his fishing. And when you get advice that conflicts with some you got elsewhere, just keep quiet, eh? Don't say, 'Oh, but only the other day, Bill Bloggs said what you just told me was all wrong!' If you do, you may get told to beggar off and find Bill Bloggs!

You will certainly receive conflicting advice, and then you have to use your own judgement to decide which to take. Remember that there are more ways than one of catching fish, even in the same conditions on the same water. I've sat in a boat with a friend who was knocking out fish with a black lure on a Hi-D line, while I was picking them off with a floating daddy-long-legs. Both methods were right on that day.

There's one thing you can depend on, though: if another chap you see at the waterside is catching fish, then his fly and method must be among the correct ones for that time and place. You fish the same fly in the same way and you must be in with a chance of fish. But when you ask, don't just find out what fly pattern. You want to know what sort of line, how much sinking time to allow, what speed and type of retrieve to use. Ask, and you'll be told. Believe it!

Casting and Accuracy

Much has been written about distance casting in trout fly-fishing, little about accuracy, yet there are many situations where the latter is the more important.

It is obviously so in river fishing, where you may need to drop a dry fly accurately to a rising fish or offer a nymph to a fish you can see feeding below the surface. On rain-fed rivers watercraft that tells an angler where a trout is most likely to lie is useless without the ability to put the fly in that place.

On large lakes and reservoirs, the need for accuracy may be less obvious. The late Major Oliver Kite described stillwater trout fishing thus: 'You chuck it out, you pull it in, and when you can't you've got one!' Much stillwater trout fishing is done in exactly that way, specially when sunk lines and large lures are used. It is true that for such fishing to be successful, much needs to be known about sinking rates, retrieve rates, timing the strike, and so on, but accurate placement of the fly in casting is seldom necessary.

There are, however, many opportunities on the big stillwaters for surface fishing, either with a dry fly or a fly just beneath the surface, when rises by trout, or water disturbances caused by feeding trout, can be seen. Then, the highest degree of accuracy is called for, because the fly has to be placed correctly both in space and in time.

The dry-fly fisherman on a typical chalk-stream sees a rising trout and moves into position. When he has done so, the distance and direction of the fish are fixed. Provided he does not scare it, he can cast again and again. His casting requirement does not alter. On a stillwater, a feeding fish is moving relative to the angler. Each cast has to be different both in distance and in direction, and accuracy is the more difficult to ensure.

How may it be acquired? Obviously, by practice. Many anglers nowadays fish stillwaters and most of the casting they do is at random, on the basis that Oliver Kite described. They cast repeatedly in the hope that a trout will come along and take the fly as it is retrieved. Often enough, one does. Often enough, the angler can do nothing else. But if he wants to cast accurately when the occasion demands it I suggest he should still strive for it when it is unnecessary. Let every throw be aimed at something. A floating leaf, a piece of alga, a patch of foam: always aim your fly at a target of some kind, every time you make a cast.

Accuracy can be improved by suitable tackle. A rod performs best when the right weight of line is aerialised. So you must provide your rod with a line size that will give it the right load at the range to which you expect to cast. But, you will say, I cast at all sorts of different ranges! So you do; but if you fish a river 10 yd wide, you will seldom aerialise more than 7 or 8 yd of line. In those circumstances, you will be wise to use a line one size heavier than that recommended by the rod maker, who bases his recommendations on the assumption that the length of line aerialised will be 10 yd.

At the other extreme, you may fish a water where you need the best accuracy you can get at ranges of 18–20 yd. Then you would be wise to use a fly line one or even two sizes less than that recommended for your rod, because to reach 20 yd you will aerialise 14 yd of line, not just 10. Remember, you have around 2½ yd of rod and perhaps 3½ yd of leader.

You can forget about accuracy at distances beyond 20 yd. Even at that range, if you put your fly within a couple of feet of your aiming point, it's a happy fluke. You probably don't believe me. All right, go out on a lawn. Measure – don't guess – 20 yd, and place a tin can and a friend with some pegs at that distance. Cast at the can, and get your friend to stick in a peg where your fly falls, cast after cast. Then walk up and look at those pegs. See how many are within a couple of feet of the can. See how many are 4 or 5 ft, or more, away. Then console yourself with the thought that in the tournament accuracy event, the farthest target is 13 ½ yd from the casting platform; it is 2 ½ ft in diameter, and the world's best casters don't always hit it.

Don't use too long a leader. Nowadays one hears much about leaders 15 ft long, sometimes even 20 ft. The idea is that fly line scares trout, but nylon doesn't. One could argue about whether that is wholly true, but even supposing it is, the object of the long leader is defeated if it falls in a heap, which all too commonly happens with very long leaders. The longest leader with which I can cast accurately is about 10 ft, consisting of a knotless taper with about 12 in of heavy nylon between its butt and the end of the fly line.

And the leader must relate to the fly. It has to be heavier if it is to straighten properly with a big winged mayfly, having high air resistance, attached. In an adverse wind, the leader has to be shortened to retain accuracy. You may have to reduce it to as short as 6 or 7 ft.

In stillwater fishing, you may have to change your casting direction. The secret of this is to point your rod at your new target before lifting off into the back-cast. Barrie Welham gave me that tip and it has proved invaluable.

Perhaps the greatest need for accuracy comes when you want to catch one of those outsize rainbows that are to be found in some still waters. When you see something resembling a small airship gliding along within casting range, near enough is not good enough. These great fish seldom deviate from their chosen course to take a real insect, let along an artificial one. You have to cast your fly so that it sinks right in front of their noses – at the right time. Cast too far ahead and it will have sunk too deep. Not far enough, and the big fish glides underneath it.

Random casting won't do in this kind of fishing. The big fish are in a tiny minority. There are plenty of smaller, more active ones, and if you cast at random those will be what you will catch. Every trout I have caught over 7 lb was a fish I saw and cast to, as accurately as possible, with two exceptions: one a Kennet fish caught while I was coarse fishing and the other a big fish that took a dead dace in a lake. I have only hooked one monster trout by casting a fly at random, and that one shed the hook.

If you want to catch a really big trout, and have access to waters holding such fish, the two essentials are ability to see the fish, sometimes in water that is not very clear; and the accuracy of casting that places your fly exactly right relative to the fish you see. Choice of fly, method of retrieve, and the rest are of secondary importance. If you can't see them, you're most unlikely to catch them. Even if you can see them, you're still unlikely to catch them unless you drop your fly just right. Just right means within a few inches, and it is constant practice with suitable tackle that gives you that kind of accuracy. I repeat, even when there are no fish to cast at, always cast at something. Let every cast be an aimed cast. Then, when a really accurate cast is essential, you are much more likely to produce it.

Fly Lines

Since the expansion in stillwater trout fishing that commenced in Britain in the middle 1960s, there has been a great proliferation of fly-line types and a positive spate of articles about the use and value of those available. We have floaters, floaters with sink-tips, neutral-densities, slow, medium and fast sinkers, and even lead-core lines.

Very curious notions about how these various lines behave seem to be commonly held. I am frequently told by anglers that they have been fishing at depths of 10, 15, or even 20 ft, when I know from watching them that their flies have never gone more than a couple of feet below the surface, and often less than half of that.

If a retrieve, even one of modest speed, is begun within a few seconds of the line alighting on the surface, an unleaded fly on a floating line, a sink tip, a neutral-density line, or even a slow sinker, will never go down as much as a foot. The sinking rate of the Scientific Anglers' Wet-Cell I, a slow sinker, is about 1 ft in seven seconds for the size 8 line; a little less with lower sizes and little more with heavier ones.

The leader, however, sinks more slowly than the line; so if the angler begins his retrieve after about seven seconds, the fly will be about 3–9 in down, depending on the nature of its dressing. And it will not go any deeper once the retrieve has started.

With lines of even lower specific gravity, like floaters, sink-tips and neutral-densities, the fly will come up towards the surface once the retrieve begins.

Even with quite heavily leaded flies, which may sink deeply in a few seconds, any but the slowest retrieve brings them within a short distance of the surface, within a few yards of the start of the retrieve. A fast retrieve with a floating line will bring a fly carrying a whole swan-shot up to within a few inches of the surface.

There is virtually no difference in the depth at which an unleaded fly fishes, between straightforward floating lines and sink-tips. The only virtue in the latter type of line that I can discover is that it submerges the leader during the first 2 or 3 yd of the retrieve, or by the action of the current in river fishing. Since floating leaders have a disastrous fish-scaring effect, this probably accounts for successful catches being made by anglers who have changed from plain floaters to sink-tips; but there are other ways of ensuring that the leader sinks, as by treating it with a mixture of fuller's earth, detergent and glycerine, or a proprietary preparation like Permasink.

As against the possible advantage of the sink-tip lines in getting the leader below the surface, there is the fact that such lines seem to cast badly. Perhaps my casting is at fault, but I can never seem to cast smoothly and accurately with a sink-tip line. If I want to fish a heavily weighted fly very deep, I tie in an appropriate length of heavy monofil between the end of a floating fly-line and the butt of my tapered leader.

While the thicker part of the modern plastic-coated floating fly line is quite buoyant, if kept clean, the thin end of the taper is barely capable of floating. It takes very little to make it sink. A coat of paint, the sort they sell for painting plastics, with a little powdered lead stirred into it, suffices. This can be applied to a longer or shorter length of line, as you wish.

Anyone who has been involved, directly or indirectly, in a court case where witnesses have been asked to state how long it took something to happen, will realise how wildly inaccurate is the average person's guess about such matters. For example, when one has a very big fish hooked, seconds seem almost like minutes, and I have often been amazed, when I look at my stop-watch, to find that what seemed like a quarter of an hour was actually only three or four minutes.

That is why I recommend anyone who uses sinking lines in still waters to acquire a watch with a second-hand, and to use it to fix the time allowed for the line to sink. It is useful to know something about the sinking rate of the line one is using, but figures can be only approximate, since they depend not only on the specific gravity of the line but also on its size and the length in the water, as well as the water resistance of the fly in use. I can therefore offer only a very rough guide that applies to one manufacturer's products: the Scientific Anglers' Wet-Cel I, Wet-Cel II and Hi-D lines in size 8 have these sinking rates: 1 ft, in seven seconds, 1 ft in five seconds and 1 ft in three seconds respectively, when about 10 yd is in the water. In each case, lighter lines sink more slowly, heavier ones more quickly, but the difference is not very great.

Except for leaded flies, the fly sinks more slowly than the line, and when fishing really deep the leader will be vertical, the fly above the end of the line. When the angler starts his retrieve, the fly accelerates in a downward direction, while the heaviest part of the line rises only slowly. The path of the fly is thus curved and it only reaches its greatest depth, always less than that reached by the line, when upwards of a third of the retrieve has taken place. I assume, of course, that a sufficiently long throw has been made to make this fly-path possible; obviously, if you are trying to fish 30 ft deep and cast only 30 ft, the line and fly can never reach the required depth, or even come near to it.

A useful rule of thumb for deep fishing is that you must cast at least three times the depth at which you want to fish, otherwise your fly will spend little or no time at the depth required. Even with a 30 yd cast, you cannot fish a fly for more than about 10 yd of the retrieve at a depth of 30 ft, and still keep in effective touch with your fly.

How deep it is necessary or desirable to fish depends on conditions. I am sure a great deal of fishing with sinking lines is done on lakes and reservoirs when a floater would be more successful. When there is no sign of surface activity by the fish, it is often better to use the floating line and a leaded fly than to change to a sinking line. There are, however, times when all the fish are down very deep, usually after several days of hot weather, and then the sinking line is essential. At Hanningfield, our sonar once showed fish nearly 40 ft down; fish at up to 30 ft are commonly located in such conditions.

The sinking line is also advantageous for fast retrieves; it causes no surface disturbance as does a floating line.

For seeking outsize brown trout on fly-only lakes and large reservoirs, the sinking line has to be used most of the time, and one special method has proved effective for these fish. It involves a Hi-D line and a leader only about 9 in long, to which is attached a Rasputin or similar very buoyant fly. After allowing ample sinking time, enough for the line to lie on the bottom, the retrieve is made very slowly indeed, with frequent pauses. The big brown trout mainly feed at the bottom, though not below the thermocline. Depths of from 8 to 25 ft may prove productive. The warmer the water, the deeper it pays to fish for these big brown trout.

I have omitted mention of any methods of fishing with lead-core lines, which I find awkward and potentially dangerous to cast. They are undoubtedly effective, especially when trailed behind a moving boat, but while I would be sorry to see them banned from the big reservoirs, their use can only by a long stretch be called fly-fishing, and I don't find it very entertaining even when it is successful.

Tackle Improvements

Notwithstanding the few who cry 'Unsporting!' whenever an improvement in fishing tackle is made, most anglers welcome progress in the design, material and manufacture of the rods, reels, lines and other tackle items they can buy. In the last quarter-century there have been many advances. Split cane gave place first to glass fibre and then to carbon fibre. There have been useful improvements in rod rings; plastic-coated lines have replaced silk and linseed oil. Nylon is used instead of silkworm gut, and there have been advances in other fields, including the design of artificial flies.

Not all changes have been for the better. No one has produced a synthetic leader material that is as good as silkworm gut. Nylon is more convenient, considerably cheaper, and less prone to rotting and fraying, but it doesn't cast nearly as well. That is because it is lighter and stiffer, for a given thickness, than well-soaked gut.

Hooks, generally speaking, are greatly inferior to those produced a hundred years ago. I say this with certainty since I have some hundred-year-old hooks. I surmise that they were made by leather-aproned craftsmen using hard-won skill and knowledge, and at the time they were sold they cost a great deal more in real terms than modern hooks.

Now why, at a time when we can send men to the moon and back, should we have to use inferior fish hooks and inferior leader material?

The answer, as I see it, lies in a combination of attitudes and quantities.

Hooks are made of straight carbon steel, as they were a century ago. If you harden and temper that sort of steel correctly, it is as good as a complex alloy steel, but it is highly critical of errors in the hardening and tempering process.

My job is in the technical side of the lawn-mower business; we make high-performance mowers for cutting large areas of grass, and that means we have to know about steel. We can use complex alloy steels, because enough of these steels is bought to make their use possible in the form we want. The steel-makers are quite happy to produce 50 tons of mower blades in an alloy like EN11 or EN45. But the world's entire fish hook-making businesses don't use enough steel to justify a single melt.

Nobody wants 50 tons of EN45 alloy steel wire. The only wire hook-makers can get is straight carbon steel, like they use for needles and other applications. The alloy steels are very tolerant of quite large errors in heat treatment when they are hardened and tempered. If we could get hook-making wire in a suitable alloy steel, every hook would be a good one.

As it is, they aren't and it is difficult to see what can be done about it.

I think it very likely that scientists who understand plastics could easily produce a material that would be much better for leaders than nylon. But where would they find the volume sales that would justify the research and the capital investment in production plant? The ladies are not interested in heavier and more flexible tights. Nobody wants heavier ropes. How many pounds of nylon are used in fly-fishing leaders?

We have been lucky with carbon fibre. Had its use been confined only to rod manufacture, nobody would own a carbon fibre rod. As it is, the material is used in aircraft engines, parts of aircraft and racing car structures, in rowing boats, oars, in skis, in golf club shafts and in vaulting poles, as well as other applications. The total volume is enough to finance the production of carbon fibre, of which only a small fraction goes to make fishing rods.

Even this is not ideal. If the demand were sufficient, we could use better weaves of cloth for wrapping mandrels to produce rod blanks, incorporating varying grades of carbon, glass and perhaps boron fibres so as to have the best elastic modulus in every part of a rod – lower near the tip, higher near the butt.

That may come with time, specially if some much larger consumer than the tackle industry wants material of that kind.

It seems likely that room for improvement also exists in fly-line coatings, that can be filled only if a demand occurs for a plastic for some other purpose where larger quantities are required. This is the trouble in tackle; the quantities needed are so small. How many fly-lines can you coat with all the PVC that goes into making just one plastic bucket?

There is one field, however, where we can make progress without incurring any cost whatever, in view of which it is surprising to see how few anglers take advantage. This is knots. The Grinner and Double Grinner knots are demonstrably stronger than Blood and Half-Blood knots, even when the latter are tucked. They are easier to tie, equally neat, and very much more reliable because their ends are trapped under all the knot turns, instead of being jammed between adjacent turns, from where they can all too easily slip.

This fact also allows the joining of strands of quite considerably different thickness. So in every possible respect, these are better knots, yet I hardly ever come across an angler who uses them. The treacherous Blood and Half-Blood knots are still preferred.

Since aluminium alloy replaced brass for fly reels, there has been relatively little progress. Magnesium is 25 per cent lighter than aluminium and nearly as strong, but it is much more difficult to protect against corrosion, and some manufacturers and their insurance companies are scared of it, since the turnings and swarf when it is being machined can, if proper care is not taken, ignite and burn with great fury. Having experienced a lathe fire when I was turning the drum of a reel, with no serious consequences, I do not share these fears, though the fire was dramatic and impressive.

Magnesium certainly offers useful savings in weight, and I expect to see it used more, now that the importance of not using heavy reels on light carbon-fibre rods is more widely appreciated. Whether carbon-fibre-reinforced plastic will ever replace metal in fly-reels is not so likely. The examples so far produced have not impressed me; the saving in weight is trivial in respect of the much higher cost.

If we want fibre-reinforced plastic reels, what's wrong with fibreglass? It's just as strong as carbon-fibre, and although it isn't as stiff, it's stiff enough not to bend much in the shape and size of components you'd put into a fly-reel. In fact, you could use a more rigid sort of plastic. There's nothing new about this; before the war, reels made of Bakelite were in steady production, and they weren't even reinforced!

What I expect to see in the next decade is small but useful improvements using the same materials we now have and have learned to know, but whether we do or not, better tackle will never make bad anglers into good ones.

Hooks and Holding Power

The matter of hook size gives rise to differences of opinion among trout-fishers. Some hold that, given sufficient skill, even the tiniest hooks suffice to land large trout. Others believe that the use of very small hooks gives rise to an unreasonable proportion of lost fish, and that the use of such hooks is positively unsportsmanlike. A third view is that it is wrong to use flies dressed on hooks larger than some particular size; for example, at Peckhams's Copse in Sussex and at Packington, there is a rule forbidding the use of a hook larger than ½ in from eye to bend, which in the case of a normally shaped hook means No 12.

At Two Lakes, the limit on hook size is No 8, which seems to me more realistic. Presumably, the object of limiting hook-size is to discourage the use of artificials that imitate fish rather than insects, though it is easy enough to tie fish-imitating lures on small hooks. To insist on a maximum hook-size of No 12 does, however, inhibit the fly-dresser who wishes to imitate some of the larger aquatic insects, like the great red sedge, the mayflies and the larvae of damsel flies, dragonflies and water-beetles, as well as some terrestrial insects like the crane-flies.

Does the use of very small hooks lead to too many fish being lost? It seems to me to depend very much upon the nature of a trout fishery, and of the fish it contains. There are two kinds of trout from which very small hooks seem especially prone to come adrift: fresh-run sea trout and rainbow trout that have grown particularly quickly. In my experience, hooks in the range 12 to 20 or smaller do tend to come away all too easily from such fish, and the smaller the hook, the more likely are these kinds of trout to be lost. On the other hand, small hooks usually secure very reliable holds on brown trout and on the rainbow trout that one finds in typical chalk streams. I can recollect only one case in the last three seasons of my losing a trout through hook-hold failure in streams of this kind, though I seldom use a hook larger than 12 and frequently fish small dry flies and nymphs down to size 18.

It has to be remembered that in order to fish any fly properly, the thickness of the leader point has to be correctly related to the size of the fly. The smaller the hook, the thinner and weaker the leader point must be. Therefore, the matter does not end with the security of the hook-hold.

A small hook may secure a most reliable hold in the mouth of a brown trout, but if the fly is attached via a leader point that breaks at, say, 1½ or 2 lb, then the risk of breakage must be higher by far than it would have been had the same fish been hooked on a fly that allowed the use of a leader capable of standing a 4- or 5-lb pull. Exactly how great the risk is, with leader strengths appropriate to tiny hooks, depends to a large extent upon the skill and knowledge of the angler. I am well convinced that trout are not scared by being hooked on small hooks. It is by no means rare for an angler to break at the strike, and for the fish he struck to continue feeding. What does scare a hooked trout is the pull of the line and/or the sight of the angler. Either will cause the fish to seek shelter in weed or snags, or to indulge in tackle-straining runs or leaps.

If the angler is able to remain concealed both before and after he has hooked his fish, and takes care to apply only the right amount of pressure, he can keep the fish moving sufficiently to tire it without alarming it to the extent of producing behaviour that sets his fine leader at risk. Unfortunately, this is not always possible, and one of the most common occurrences that prevents it is the arrival, at the double, of a well-meaning friend, pounding along the bank in full view of the fish and brandishing a landing net. I have even known river-keepers, who ought to know better, to behave in this way.

All this applies to river-fishing, where trout are hooked on comparatively short lines. In lake and reservoir-fishing, circumstances are usually quite different. The bank angler is usually casting a much longer line, and even if this is a floating kind it is quickly drowned when a trout is hooked. The fish is then pulling against the drag of the submerged line, which, as anyone knows who has tried to lift a sunken line straight into a back-cast, can be very great. Of course the trout is greatly alarmed at feeling this drag and sets off at high speed, quickly submerging any of the fly line that was previously on the surface or in the air. That further increases drag, which is in any case greatly increased by the fact that the fish is going faster. Drag increases with the square of the speed; if the fish goes twice as fast, the line-drag is multiplied by four.

This is why trout hooked in lakes and reservoirs so often run at very high speeds and for great distances. Most habitual reservoir trout-fishers have encountered fish that have taken out 60 or 70 yd of line in a single tearing run, ending in a head-shaking leap. Since many of these fish are rainbow trout that have grown very fast and thus have tender mouths, it is not surprising that losses, either through hook-hold failure or leader breakage, are common where very small hooks and fine leader points are used.

It may be mentioned at this point that the much-maligned shooting head system, where instead of the usual 30 yd of dressed fly-line, only 10–12 yd, attached to monofilament backing, are used, does reduce very considerably the risk of breakage or failure of hook-holds with small flies, because it reduces line-drag. The drag of 10 yd of fly-line, being pulled along underwater, is only a third of what it would be with a full line of 30 yd. Since it is manifestly detrimental to any trout fishery for large numbers of fish to be hooked and lost, and since there are many trout-fishers who deprecate the use of large lures, one might think that the shooting-head system would be encouraged.

It has certainly made it possible for me to catch both brown and rainbow trout upwards of 5-lb in weight on hooks as small as No 16 and on leader points of nominal 3-lb b.s., which would inevitably have escaped had I been using full 30-yd fly-lines.

One further point that tends to confuse the issue of hook size is that of hook quality. Nowadays, it is difficult to obtain really reliable hooks, and obviously, the smaller the hook, the more disastrous will be any shortcomings in quality. This alone has undoubtedly caused many anglers to think that very small hooks lose too many fish. I am quite unable to purchase hooks that, size for size and in similar wire-thickness, are nearly as good as some hooks I have that are more than a century old. If hook-makers would only accept the fact that anglers generally will willingly pay more for first-class hooks, we could all use smaller sizes, where appropriate, with much greater confidence.

Leaders

I read with interest a magazine article by Peter Lapsley, on the subject of leaders. I am always happy to debate with Peter because both of us are willing to be convinced, and neither is afraid to concede that he has been mistaken.

There are assumptions in Peter's article that seem to me to be dubious, to say the least.

To begin with, good leader turnover is affected by so many factors that to analyse it is well-nigh impossible. Among these factors are velocity, mass, air resistance, wind direction and speed, flexibility of the nylon, weight distribution along the leader.

As usual, when we consider these factors, we find conflicts. A heavier leader will have greater momentum but it will have higher air resistance and lower flexibility. I've been fishing for a very long time: at least twenty years before nylon was invented. Then we used silkworm gut, and although that had disadvantages by comparison with nylon, it had also some quite positive advantages.

It soaked up a lot of water, which made it much heavier than nylon for any given thickness. When it was well soaked, it was also much more flexible than nylon. Flexibility is important for two reasons: it produces a tighter loop as the leader unrolls, and it allows a more flexible movement of the fly. So despite the tendency to rot and to become frayed, silkworm gut enabled us to fish very effectively. Its advantages are unobtainable with nylon or other kinds of man-made monofil.

One thing that I recall from the days of silkworm gut: the most popular length for ready-made tapered gut leaders was 6 ft. A few people used 7½ or 9 ft, but 6 ft was usual. This tradition is pursued to some extent even now; the usual length for knotless tapered nylon leaders is 7½ or 9 ft. Of course they do not perform nearly as well as gut. We caught plenty of fish, in all sorts of water, on 6-ft leaders, and I wonder if the very long nylon leaders that are now advocated really offer much advantage. I find them very difficult to handle in a headwind or a crosswind, and I very seldom use a leader longer than 10 ft.

It would seem that Peter supports Brian Clarke's assertion that the leader should be three times as long as the depth at which the fly is desired to fish. In fact this is complete nonsense; the length of the leader has very little effect on the depth at which a fly will fish. There are two things that have a far greater effect: the weight of the fly and the rate of retrieve. With a light fly, for example a midge pupa dressed on a No 12 or 14 hook, it takes only a very little in the way of speed of retrieve to bring the fly up to within an inch of the surface, as I have discovered by practical experiment. Even a slight breeze acting on a floating line will pull the fly fast enough to bring it high in the water, even if the angler doesn't retrieve at all. The length of the leader has very little effect.

The only way to make a fly fish deep with a floating line is to make the fly heavy, either by using a heavy hook or by building copper wire or lead into the dressing. And it takes a surprising amount of lead or copper to keep a fly well down, even with a retrieve of modest pace. I say with certainty that very few anglers using floating lines ever succeed in fishing more that 3 or 4 ft deep, however long their leaders may be. Most of the time, with unleaded flies, they are fishing only inches deep and the splash that often occurs directly a fish is hooked provides confirmation of this. At the rate that most anglers retrieve sunk flies on still waters, not even a BB shot pinched on the leader would get the fly down more than a couple of feet.

The trouble with people, and specially anglers, is that they'll believe what they want to believe, and avoid carrying out the simple experiments that could establish the truth. When I suspected that popular beliefs about the depth at which flies would fish on leaders of various lengths were mistaken, I persuaded various friends to cast where, in clear water, I could see their flies, and I know now what they do or don't do. I recommend similar experiments to anyone else who wants to know.

How important the flexibility of the leader point is will depend on the size, weight and water resistance of the fly. I don't believe that the actual thickness has much bearing; trout see 2-lb points as easily as 6-lb points, but the effect of stiffness on the fly's behaviour is quite important. As Peter says, the difference in diameter between 4-lb and 6-lb nylon is fairly marginal. It is in fact about 0.002 of an inch. But

21

the difference in stiffness is far from marginal. As 6-lb nylon is about two and a half times stiffer than 4-lb nylon, that could produce a drastic difference to the underwater movement of an imitative fly pattern of modest size, like a midge pupa, sedge pupa or ephemerid nymph. It can also affect greatly the behaviour of a dry pattern fished across varying surface currents.

Most of my trout fishing is done with a knotless tapered leader designated 0x or 1x. A piece of 25-lb b.s. nylon is needle-knotted to the fly-line. I have to cut off a bit of the knotless taper I use because for some curious reason the thing is double-tapered as supplied, and I have to cut off not only the loop, but all of the back-taper. What remains is knotted to the 25-lb b.s. short-level bit, so I now have a leader about 10 ft long. If the point becomes too short and thick from fly-changing, I attach an extra level point, except where there are very big fish. Then I replace the entire knotless taper.

Because the Double Grinner knot allows lengths that differ by several thousandths of an inch in thickness to be safely joined, I can choose my point strength to suit the fly over quite a range. 0x is about 0.011 in thick; I can safely attach a piece of 0.009 in to this, about 5-lb b.s. To a 1x leader, I can attach 0.008 in, about 4-lb b.s., and at a pinch 0.007 in, which is about as fine as I ever need to go on stillwaters. I carry a few 2x and 3x leaders for river fishing where trout aren't very large, or for grayling fishing, and spools of level down to 2½-lb b.s., and with this complement of leaders and leader materials, I don't find any trout or grayling fishing for which I am handicapped.

I was surprised to find Peter Lapsley still favouring the very unreliable Half-Blood knot for attaching flies. I used it for many years, and when, after losing a fish and a fly, I saw a little corkscrew-end to my leader point, I assumed I had tied the knot badly. Now I know better. All Blood and Half-Blood knots are treacherous, however carefully and correctly you tie them. Grinners and Double Grinners are just as easily tied and totally reliable, as well as being just as neat as Blood and Half-Blood knots.

Whether knots assist much in achieving better turnover of the leader, I am inclined to doubt. What matters is weight, and the extra length of nylon involved in two or three knots is infinitesimal compared to the total weight of the leader. The belief that the weight of the knots helps probably stems from the fact that a knotted leader has better weight distribution than a level or a knotless tapered leader. What we need is a knotless taper that is steeper than those currently available, so that the length of thicker stuff is greater, followed by a faster taper towards the point. This, of course, is what Peter is driving at in his leader designs, but using points cut from available knotless tapers is a very expensive way of achieving it, and I wouldn't dream of trying to fish with the 15- and 20-ft leaders Peter recommends.

A few years back, Brian Clarke complimented me in one of his articles on the distance, accuracy and delicacy I was achieving at Latimer. He seemed surprised that I did it with a shooting head. On that day I caught about 20 fish and released most of them, a special concession on that day, having waived both bag limit and the rule saying that all fish caught had to be killed. That was with my usual 10-ft leader.

More recently, Peter Lapsley saw me catch some fish at Avington, and he may remember that the fly alighted with satisfactory delicacy and accuracy, with adequate leader turnover. So I shall persist with my present leaders until I hear more convincing reasons for making a change than those so far given.

I will, however, add that I take Peter's point about the best place for a break to occur. If some enterprising nylon maker could offer us point material consisting of 4- or 5-ft lengths of knotless taper, from which we would cut suitable 2-ft points for all occasions, at a good deal lower price than the present 7½ and 9-ft double-tapered leaders with useless loops tied in them, many of us would be very grateful.

End of the Mayfly

Most of the books about trout fishing that deal with mayfly refer to a difficult period for the fly-fisher after the mayfly period has ended. This is usually ascribed to the trout having been glutted with food while the mayfly was hatching, and it is an explanation for the lean spell which most trout-fishers with whom I have discussed the matter would seem to accept.

I do not. Trout in fish farms that are regularly fed with as much as they can eat do not cease feeding for weeks at a time. A trout that has eaten as much as its stomach can hold will have digested all the food within 24 hours or so, and will be ready for more. The explanation for difficult fishing from mid-June onwards must surely lie elsewhere, and I am sure it involves more than one factor.

Waters that produce large mayfly hatches must be suitable for these insects, whose nymphs live in burrows in sandy silt. The nature of this silt is fairly critical; it has to be sufficiently stable so that it is not scoured away by increases in flow after rain or from other causes. It has to be to some extent permeable and it must hold enough organic matter to feed the mayfly nymphs. It seems to me likely that rivers, or stretches of river, that provide suitable mayfly environments are less suitable for some other aquatic insects and particularly those species which on other waters are most in evidence from mid-June onwards. Other organisms that enjoy an environment similar to that preferred by the mayfly may consist of insects that hatch later in the year, and of such creatures as fresh-water shrimps and lamprey larvae that do not hatch at all, but induce the trout to feed at or near the bed of the river.

The sandy silt favoured by the mayfly is also an environment suitable for a number of kinds of caddis larvae. These larvae predate heavily upon the eggs and young nymphs of non-burrowing ephemerid species and may, where present in large numbers, substantially reduce the quantity of small fly that hatches, while themselves increasing the inducement to the trout to feed at the bottom of the river. It is worth remembering here that by eating large numbers of caddis, the bigger grayling contribute to the quantity of ephemerid fly, and therefore, on rivers where dry-fly fishing is the preferred method, it may be inadvisable to cull grayling stocks too heavily – especially where there are large mayfly hatches.

There are other factors that may contribute to difficult fishing and reduced catches after the mayfly period. On well-fished waters, not only are many trout caught during the mayfly time, but also, many are hooked and lost, pricked, or caught and returned. The result of all this, unless restocking is carried out, is a river holding fewer trout, many of which have been taught how to avoid capture. I do not subscribe to the view that a trout is a reasoning animal, but it is able to relate cause and effect to an extent sufficient to make it a good deal harder to catch after being once hooked.

A third factor that may take effect as the trout-fishing season progresses is increased water temperature, which inhibits activity by the trout, and specially by brown trout, until some cooling takes place in the evening. Many species of fish are similarly affected and the coarse-fish angler knows very well that in the first three months of his fishing season, which starts on 16 June, the very time when mayfly hatches are ending, his best chances of success are late in the evening, through the night, and in the early morning.

Provided stocks of trout have not been too seriously reduced before mid-June, it is still possible to make satisfactory catches from that time onwards by the use of different tactics, though it must be admitted that a dry-fly-only rule imposes a very serious handicap, limiting the angler's opportunities to the very occasional hatch of small fly in the daytime and the use of sedge or large moth imitations at dusk.

Where the rules are more liberal, however, fish may be taken through the day by means of nymphs, artificial fresh-water shrimps and imitations of sedge pupae. In deep fast water, it is necessary to build underbodies of lead for these patterns so as to get them down near the bottom where the trout are usually feeding. As well as using leaded patterns, it may also be necessary to employ special techniques for fishing them, by casting upstream curves, a snaky line, or by making an upstream mend as in greased-line fishing for salmon. In all cases the object is to avoid line-drag while the weighted fly is sinking.

In all this, the ability to see fish that are deep in the water is a tremendous asset. It is capable of being learned and should be practised, not least because the angler who uses deep-fishing tactics may be accused of raking the water and thus catching numbers of immature fish. In practice, the patterns used for deep fishing are quite large, tied on hooks of sizes 10 and 8, and for some reason do not attract small fish very often, possibly because such fish seldom occupy lies in deeper water. Nevertheless, if one can actually see trout, their size can be judged, and should it appear insufficient, they can be let alone.

Certain steps can be taken to make seeing fish easier, as by wearing headgear with a broad brim or peak, and polarised spectacles; by taking care to avoid looking at the sky or at bright reflections in the water; and by spending plenty of time looking into likely places. It is often surprising how, in an area of water that appears barren at the first glance, a concentrated examination taking several minutes will reveal the presence of a good fish.

By these means, satisfactory sport may be enjoyed after the mayfly season has ended and the more orthodox ways of fly-fishing have ceased to provide much of it. One compensation for the increased difficulties is the fact that trout at this time are in the peak of condition, with both their fighting and culinary qualities at their best.

Fishing Coloured Water

In a magazine article, D. Macer Wright mentioned the algal growths that often occur in lakes. Sometimes these growths are so extensive that visibility is greatly limited; when the hand is immersed as far as the wrist, one cannot see the tips of the fingers.

Catching trout in these conditions is difficult, simply because the fish cannot see very far. They are unlikely to take a fly they do not see.

Fortunately, there are ways in which the angler can increase his chances of catching fish when algal growth is thick.

If the fish cannot be seen to be feeding on any particular insect or other organism, and when the surface is seldom broken by rises, it is wise to use a fly pattern that is so coloured as to be visible at the greatest possible distance in the murk, and which is so designed as to be suitable for fishing at a very slow rate of retrieve, so that should it become visible to a trout, it will remain within visible range for a longer time.

I deduce from considerable practical trial that the colours that trout can see at the greatest distance are orange and yellow.

Without wishing to be too technical, it is a fact, in engineering, that the stiffness of any structure supported at one end only will vary inversely with the cube of the length, if the cross-section is constant. The application of this principle to fly design is that a small increase in the length of a hackle fibre, or a hair in a wing, will produce a great increase in its flexibility. To give a simple example, if you tie in a hair wing twice as long, it will be eight times as flexible.

Flexibility is exactly what we want in flies that are to be moved very slowly. We can obtain it either by tying flies with fibres and hairs much longer than usual, or by choosing exceptionally flexible materials, like marabou or very fine hair.

An example of a very effective fly for murky water is Mrs Palmer. It is tied on a No 8 long-shank hook and has a wing of pale primrose goat hair, twice as long as the hook. Its drawback is that if very long casting is attempted with it, the wing too often becomes caught under the bend of the hook; but fortunately, long casting is unnecessary in murky water, because the fish do not easily see the angler on the bank, specially against the sky.

I well remember the first time I used this pattern at Two Lakes, on a day when the water was exceptionally rich in algae. The fly was drawn very slowly indeed, just under the surface. I could see it all the time, and fish after fish loomed out of the murk and annexed it. Since then it has caught me many a fish in similar conditions. Unfortunately this fly is often offered for sale with a wing extending only as far as the hook-bend, which destroys the entire principle of the design.

A fly tied similarly but with hot orange hair also does well, and I am inclined to think that if the murk is olive to brown, the yellow fly is the better choice, while when the water is green, the orange pattern does better.

Trout can not only see; they can also detect vibrations. To produce vibrations, a fly can be tied with stiff, wound cock hackles, and fished sunk. If this is pulled in a series of jerks, the hackles produce vibrations that will attract trout. I have lately used an unnamed pattern, which consists of a dubbed body of fluorescent arc-chrome wool, tied fat, with a tail of white fluorescent wool, and two ginger cock hackles wound at the head and in the centre of the body, giving a silhouette resembling that of a Dambuster or a single-hook Worm fly. The hook is a No 8 long-shank, and the pattern has been very successful in algae-thick water.

The depth at which these patterns are fished will depend upon water temperature and wind. If the fish are suspected of lying deep, a sinking line will be necessary, but very often trout will come up for a fly fished just under the surface, and I suggest that usually it should be so tried, on a floating line, before the sinking line is used.

The above has been concerned with the manifest absence of surface-feeding activity. When such activity is obvious, it is almost always associated with a particular food that has to be imitated, such as midge pupae of one sort or another. Attractor flies like Mrs Palmer will not do well; indeed they will commonly catch nothing.

The most effective procedure is to lay out a floating line, terminating in a knotless tapered leader and a single fly imitating what the trout are judged to be eating. When a rise is seen within casting range, the fly is lifted off and put down as accurately and as quickly as possible, on the upwind edge of the rise-ring. The faster and more accurately this is done, the more likely the fly is to be taken. Unless the angler is almost supernaturally quick and skilful, he will not obtain an offer at every throw. An ordinary caster may, however, hook a fish after a dozen to 20 attempts and thus catch a satisfactory number of trout in a couple of hours, provided his diagnosis of the creature the trout are eating is correct and he has a reasonably good imitation of it.

It is true that trout do not invariably work upwind, and sometimes there is no wind. One can only say that where there is some breeze or drift, trout do tend to move upwind or up-drift after making a rise, more often than not. It is therefore sensible to place the fly, if possible, on the upwind edge of the rise-ring, in the absence of any other clue as to the direction in which the fish is moving, and to do so as quickly as possible. The reason for speed is that the longer the delay, the farther the trout is likely to have moved. If you can place the fly quickly enough, the trout may see it even if he has moved in an unpredicted direction, provided he has not moved too far.

If the fly is not taken after it has been pulled a foot or so, it should be left until another rise provides the target for another quick lift and throw. Half a dozen evident refusals will suggest an incorrect choice of pattern.

By these means, good catches can usually be made in water that looks too thick for successful fishing to be possible.

Selective Breeding

In his article 'Beware the fast-growing trout', Captain T.B. Thomas says that he knows nothing about genetics. I am more fortunate, having studied the subject over some seven years after the Second World War, and can thus follow what is being done in rainbow-trout breeding.

Like all other animal and plant species, rainbow trout possess what is known as a gene pool: that is, a wide range of variation in inherited characters within their species. It is the possession of such a gene pool that allows a species to be selected to suit the requirements of the livestock breeder, and permits such wide differences between breeds as we find in dogs and in horses, for example. When we consider the latter, we are struck by the difference in size between the ancestral wild horse and the modern Shetland pony or heavy shire horse.

These differences have been obtained by selective breeding; and similar results can be and have been obtained in fish breeding. In fish breeding, however, progress towards the desired type is more rapid because the rate of reproduction is much higher. A mare may produce eight foals in a decade; a hen trout may produce 20,000 eggs in one year.

Selective breeding of fish is not new. It has been practised with carp on the Continent for a long time, with quite spectacular results. The ordinary wild carp found in Britain for the last 400 years or more seldom reach 20 lb; imported strains of continental carp reach 40 lb or more. What is more important, these selectively bred strains make more than twice the growth of wild carp in the same waters.

While it is true that the ultimate size to which fish can grow is always dependent on the food supply, it is equally true that this also depends on inherited growth capacity. It is only in the very poorest waters that the fish with high inherited growth capacity will fail to do better than that with lower capacity. I expect what has been done to improve rainbows by selective breeding to benefit more than half of the waters into which they are introduced, to a very noticeable extent.

The advantage is not confined to growth rate in the waters concerned. For obvious reasons, stocking with rainbow trout is best done with fish of about 1 lb in weight. Formerly, these were fish about two years old. With the new strain, this weight can be reached in one year, halving all the fish-farm costs except feed and transport. In addition, any fish that remain uncaught will have a life expectation in river, reservoir or lake, of three years instead of only two. If they grow at all, they should be considerably larger at the end of this extended period.

There is also the matter of spawning times. For too long, spring-spawning rainbows have posed problems to fishery management; most anglers who fish waters stocked with rainbows have been all too familiar with fish taken in April and May that shed milt or ova all over the bank or boat bottom, which are quite unfit to eat, and which will die in a few weeks even if returned to the water. The new strain of rainbows spawns in November and December, at the same time as brown trout, an advantage for which we should be grateful even if there were no others.

It seems to me that many of the objections to large trout stem from the practice of some fishery managements in the past, which was to turn loose brood stock of the spring-spawning kind after these fish had been stripped and had had only a few weeks to recover. Such fish fought poorly, were not nice to eat, and usually had a rather battered appearance. A three-year-old fish of the new strain is very different, as anyone who has the fortune to hook one soon discovers.

Capt. Thomas need have no fears about whether faster-growing, uniformly autumn-spawning rainbows can be produced. It has been done. The fish are established, and any fish farmer or fishery management wishing to take advantage of the fact has the opportunity to do so, though because stocks are somewhat limited, that may not be possible for everyone this year.

There is one thing that I share with Capt. Thomas, and that is the view that one has no need to catch enormous trout to enjoy trout fishing. I have spent many happy days catching trout from waters where a half-pounder was as large as one could expect. I find the attitude of some modern anglers, that huge fish are the only ones that matter, somewhat saddening. But if we are to provide trout fishing to meet the ever-increasing demand, we shall have to do it with rainbows, because most of this fishing will be in man-made waters such as reservoirs, gravel pits and specially excavated small lakes. In such waters, brown trout are not very satisfactory, adopting a largely bottom-feeding behaviour once they reach 2 lb or so.

If we are to depend largely on rainbows, then it seems reasonable to choose the most suitable kind of rainbows: autumn spawners with high inherited growth capacity. Setting aside the effects of inflation, such fish should produce better yields at lower costs, which will benefit everyone.

Artificially Bred Trout

I began trout fishing at an early age, on a little river where the brown trout bred freely enough to eliminate the need for artificial stocking. Since then, I have fished many more waters to which the same applied.

I have also fished plenty that depended partly or entirely on artificial stocking, from quite small streams and rivers up to larger running waters, reservoirs, lochs and lakes of various sizes. It was therefore interesting to read Arthur Oglesby's article entitled 'Spring Restocking'.

It is only in recent years that the notion has been put about that artificially bred trout are tame, easy to catch and unable to fight well. This was not the view of some of the pioneers of artificial trout rearing. The famous William Lunn, river-keeper to the Houghton Club for many years, took the opposite view and so did his biographer, J.W. Hills. Pain, author of *Fifty Years on the Test*, entirely concurred with the view that hatchery trout were individually harder to catch.

My own experience will not allow me to go quite so far. It has taught me that the ease of capture and the fighting powers of artificially bred trout, as well as their palatability, are qualities about which generalisation is, to say the least of it, unwise.

One thing I do not believe is that trout can be tamed. It is true that in stewponds they become accustomed to humans on the bank who throw food to them; but this is in association with the stewpond environment. If the fish are transferred to another environment, they revert to their intuitive fear of anything on the bank that moves.

Here we have to be careful, because, believe it or not, a change to another water does not always mean a change of environment. The major feature of a stewpond full of trout is a great many trout. If large numbers of trout from such a stewpond are released at the same time and in the same place, into a fishing water, the change in environment, as far as these trout are concerned, is not apparent. It may take weeks for the consequent shoal of fish to disperse, and until they do, they will be very easy to catch, having little or no fear of anglers on the bank and taking almost any fly that may be thrown to them.

Since there are few waters that can provide food enough for a large shoal of trout, the fish tend to lose condition in the early days following their release, and consequently both their fighting qualities and their palatability are likely to suffer. Both are also dependent on how the fish were reared in the stewpond. Balanced pellet diets are now available that produce strong, red-fleshed, delicious trout, but by no means all fish farmers use them. All kinds of fish and animal wastes are minced up to feed trout in some places, and both palatability and strength may suffer.

31

Arthur Oglesby says that if stocked trout are caught before they can have taken full benefit of the natural feeding of the river, the flesh may be still pale and lean. If I found such a condition in recently supplied trout, I would soon be asking the fish farmer who supplied them what the devil he was playing at. Fish ought to leave the farm in first-class order. It is after a few weeks in waters where the food supply is inadequate that trout become pale-fleshed and lean; and if all the stock required for an entire season's fishing are dumped into the water in spring, just before fishing starts, the likelihood is that the demand for food will far exceed the supply needed to maintain the fish in good condition, a state of affairs that will persist until the majority of the stock fish have been removed.

It is easy to see where the notion has arisen that river feeding is what provides good flesh colour and fighting powers. If a river is stocked with the whole season's supply in, let us say, March, and fishing starts a month later, lots of trout will be caught that, having been on a greatly reduced diet during the interval, will be some way below top condition. As the season goes on, and more and more fish are removed, there will be more food for the survivors, especially as the natural feed increases through the late spring and summer.

At some point in time, the condition of the fish will begin to improve; and because there are now far fewer in the river – or lake – catches will fall. The fish will be less hungry and thus more discriminating; fly hatches will appear that often induce selective feeding behaviour, and there will be fewer fish anyway.

So the anglers will say, 'Aha, see how river feeding improves flesh quality and fighting powers; see how these fish have learned to avoid being caught!' The truth is, as I have explained, very different.

There is no best time to turn the entire season's stock loose in your fishery. It is wrong to release them all at the same time, whatever time that may be. All the really successful put-and-take trout fisheries I know and fish arrange their stocking on a basis of few and often. Many have their own adjacent fish farms, and restock very often indeed with a few fish at a time, well spread out in the fishery.

Each fish then experiences a true environmental change and reverts to dependence on its inherited survival instincts. Such fish are at least as difficult to catch as wild-bred ones, and because they are released in small numbers where food supplies are adequate, they do not lose condition after release.

Obviously, fisheries that have no stock-ponds of their own and depend on outside suppliers cannot stock nearly as often, but they ought to be able to break away from the once-per-season stocking system. The large reservoirs nowadays carry out monthly restocking, thus avoiding the opening-week bonanza and poor subsequent catch returns. Where adjacent stretches of river are concerned, under separate management, it should be possible by mutual agreement to organise regular stockings every four or six weeks without undue increase in the fish-farm's transport costs.

Above all, fish need spreading out. The formation, or more correctly, the perpetuation, of shoals, ought to be very carefully avoided. No doubt the driver of the hatchery truck will be anxious to dump his consignment as fast as possible and get away, and if left to himself, the whole lot will be turned loose in one place. That simply will not do. There must be some means by which the fish can be well and truly spread out to avoid shoaling.

I have seen an entire consignment of trout, all released together, form a shoal which departed downstream at high speed, and were last seen 3 miles farther down, still in a shoal and still travelling. Arthur Oglesby mentions the risk of release when a river runs high and cold. You may well lose an entire stocking in such conditions, but you are far less likely to do so if you move along the banks, dropping a few fish into each slack and backwater. If you release them in one big body, they go in a mindless mob wherever the leaders decide to swim.

And not the least of the advantages of stocking several times in the season with smaller numbers each time is that you don't put all your eggs into one basket. If the first pre-season stocking is partly lost, there will be more to come later.

Some trout farmers will grizzle at the prospect of making several trips to deliver fish, instead of one. The answer to give them is that you are willing to cover the extra cost. The improved catches of better-conditioned fish will more than compensate.

Hen Fish and Cock Fish

In the early stages of the 1967 trout-fishing season, many of the rainbow trout at Grafham were in poor condition. The hen fish were full of spawn and the cocks were dark-coloured and full of milt. By the middle of June, these 'spawny' fish had ceased to feature in our catches; but the very obvious differences between the sexes displayed by rainbows in that condition led me to take more notice of the rainbows I caught at Grafham and from other waters. I came to realise, through the rest of that season, that except during the first few weeks of the season, to catch a cock rainbow was quite rare.

Since then I have been taking notice of rainbow catches, and although I have no accurate records, I would guess that of the rainbow trout caught by anglers from lakes and reservoirs, from 80 to 90 per cent are hen fish.

This is certainly true of my own catches. The reason why I think it probable that it is also true of those made by other anglers is that I have examined carefully a very large number of photographs of trout caught from reservoirs, and in those photographs, very few cock rainbows are to be seen.

Such very capable anglers as Peter Rayment, Bob Church and Gerry Berth-Jones have sent me numerous pictures of their catches. Many pictures of catches have appeared in the angling press, and there are several in Tom Ivens's *Stillwater Fly Fishing*.

Anyone who takes the trouble to look at all the pictures he can find will, I think, form the opinion that far more hen than cock rainbows are caught by anglers. Be that so or not, I am sure everyone will agree that the matter ought to be thoroughly investigated.

The reason is, of course, that if in fact we catch four hen rainbows for every cock, then cock rainbows are costing us four times as much as hens, for practical purposes. And if, as I suspect, the ratio is even higher, say nine hens for every cock, then it means that cock rainbows are very expensive fish indeed with which to stock still-water trout fisheries.

In the days when poultry-keeping by private individuals was widespread, a similar situation occurred. People wanted laying birds, and only hens lay. It was the practice to purchase either day-old chicks or 12-week-old birds and rear them to laying age. People were not too keen to rear birds, half of which turned out to be cocks.

So they ordered females, and they got them, because by crossing certain breeds, it became possible to identify the sexes at a day old. An expert chick-sexer can make this identification with any breed or cross of poultry, but if, for example, you cross Rhode Island Reds with Light Sussex, you don't need to be an expert. If the father was a

RIR and the mother a Light Sussex, all the little female chicks are brown and all the little male chicks are pale yellow.

Nowadays, chick-sexing is a matter in which few people are concerned, but to those who are, it is even more important because if you're running a battery-laying unit holding a million birds, you don't want it half full of cocks.

Do we want our still-water trout fisheries half full of cock rainbows? I don't know what the overall recovery rate of stock fish is, but let's guess it at 30 per cent. Should we be content with a recovery rate of 3 per cent for cock rainbows, which means that if fish for stocking cost £1.87 each, a cock rainbow taken by an angler has cost, in effect, about £6?

You may ask what, if I am right about the low recovery rate of cock rainbows, is the remedy? Well, surely it is the same as with poultry, namely the separation of the sexes at the earliest possible age. We could then purchase hen fish only, for which the fish farmers would be entitled to receive a higher price. It all depends on how early in their lives the fish can be identified and separated. I believe I am right in saying that it is the feeding rather than the breeding of rainbows in a fish farm that has cost most, by the time the fish are 10–11 in long. If the sexes could be separated a few months after hatching and the males removed, the cost of feeding the females would be no more than if the sexes were mixed. The males could, perhaps, be fed on for the restaurant and hotel trade and the females sold for stocking lakes and reservoirs.

Alternatively, separation of the sexes could take place when the fish were nearly ready for distribution; of course, the job of separating the fish would cost money, but it would be worth paying more for fish offering a uniformly high recovery rate. We don't need the males for breeding, because rainbows don't breed in still waters anyway. Most of them die in their fifth year, though it is thought that a few manage to shed their eggs and survive another year.

It has been suggested that the presence of male fish is necessary to enable these few hen fish to shed. I would have thought that if it is thought desirable to encourage the survival of these fish, arrangements could be made to attract them to a part of the water where they could easily be caught and stripped artificially.

I am sure that all anglers who fish stillwaters for trout would be interested to hear the views of fish farmers and fishery managers about this question of relative recovery rates of cock and hen

35

rainbows. It would be interesting too, if I am right about far more hens being caught by anglers, whatever the reason is.

Do the hen fish feed nearer the surface, or do they eat foods that our artificial flies imitate while the cocks eat something that we don't know about? Or is there a very high death rate among cock rainbows soon after they are put into a stillwater? There must be some factor to account for far more hens than cocks being caught. My impression is that the difference in numbers is far greater on large reservoirs than on small waters, so it is possible that depth may play a part.

Although, as I said earlier, I have no exact figures, I think that there is a variation in the proportions of cock and hen rainbows that are caught through the season. In April and early May, the cocks are more in evidence, though one never catches as many cocks as hens. As the season progresses, it becomes rarer and rarer to catch cock rainbows, until September, when a few more cocks begin to feature in catches. On waters where fishing continues to the middle of October, the ratio of cocks to hens begins to approach what it was in April and early May.

What I think we need is a collection of catch records made during this and future seasons, showing the numbers of hen and cock fish taken and the dates when they were caught. We might then learn how to obtain better value for the money that is spent on stocking.

Pre-season Preparation

As a new trout season approaches, I have set down a few things I've resolved to do before it starts.

The first is to renew all the pieces of nylon that are needle-knotted to the ends of my fly-lines, and, in turn, to the thick ends of my leaders. I shall continue to use needle knots because I still don't trust the methods of gluing nylon inside a hole in the end of the fly-line with cyanoacrylate adhesive. A needle knot at the thin end of a tapered fly-line is not at all bulky.

I very rarely use more than one fly, even when fishing from a drifting boat, but for the rare occasions when I shall want to use more than one, and to provide a supply for my scrounging friends, I shall make up some leaders with droppers using Blood-Grinner knots. These knots will have a droplet of clear polyurethane varnish applied to them, to keep them dry, or at least drier. That should increase their strength by about 15 per cent.

I must tie a good supply of black midge pupae (no, I will *not* call them buzzer nymphs) with a turn or two of crimson feather fibre at their tail ends, in sizes 10 and 12. This is because, so often, there are great numbers of black midges about on still-water fisheries early in the season. The clean non-spawning fish eat these while the black spring-spawning rainbows haunt gravelly areas and snap at the large lures that anglers drag about on sinking lines. Quite a lot of anglers seem proud of catching these horrible fish, which aren't even fit to feed a cat.

I like to tie all my midge pupae with the lightest materials available: feather-fibre bodies, hackle-fibre tails and breathing tubes at the head, bronze peacock-feather herl thoraces and a hackle-stalk rib – not a metal rib. The lighter the dressing, the nearer the pupa will fish to the surface, on a retrieve of modest speed, with all the leader sunk.

My resolution is not only to avoid using white fly-lines as usual, but to fish well away from anyone else using one, specially when the sun is shining. If others like to scare trout away, they're welcome, but I shall take care they don't scare those that I'm trying to catch.

I shall use more Permagrease on floating lines in the coming season. Floating lines don't need grease to make them float, but a greased line sits *on* the surface film instead of lying *in* it, so it moves more easily across the water and lifts off with less disturbance. Before Perma-grease, line-grease removed the plasticiser from plastic-coated fly-lines, after which they cracked, but Permagrease has some plasticiser mixed into it, so it is safe to use. You just rub the line down with it, then wipe off all you can with a soft dry rag.

I wish I could find someone enterprising enough to produce little leads, cigar-shaped and with a groove along one side, for binding on to the shanks of No 8 long-shank hooks, for tying leaded mayfly and damsel-fly nymphs. Piling up seven or eight layers of wine-bottle lead foil is effective enough, but it takes time and makes these patterns expensive for anglers who have to buy from professional fly-tyers. We only need one size – or, if you want to include leaded shrimps, two or three smaller versions. In the meantime, I must get busy and top up my supply of these patterns. They're good all through the season, specially in the smaller still-water fisheries. The mayfly nymph does well in rivers, too, even where there are no natural mayflies.

Another resolution – I'm going to brush Permaflote all over my Australian bush hat, fair dinkum! Then it won't get soaked in the rain. Humans are curious creatures – they'll suffer discomfort or put up with inefficiency to avoid being laughed at, which is why so few people wear these bush hats, which are so superior to any other kind that there's really no comparison. The Australian military authorities knew what they were doing when they chose that kind of hat about seventy or eighty years ago, or perhaps even longer than that.

Talking of reluctance to look odd, why doesn't some brave soul produce a fishing jacket on the Raglan principle? We all know the problem: a waxed woven fabric lets moisture evaporate away, but gradually gets leakier and leakier, shabbier and shabbier, and costs a lot. Impervious materials like plastic or rubberised fabric keep the rain out better and continue to do so, but moisture can't escape, and on a warm day it condenses inside.

But using such fabric in the Raglan style, which involves a form of louvres, of which one could use several layers, the moisture can get out but rain can't get in, unless it falls upwards or you fish standing on your head.

I shall be doing even less wading this year, even on reservoirs. If you watch people fishing such waters, you'll find that in most places, wading only increases the distance you can put your fly from the bank by 6 or 7 yd. I've seen people wading where the bottom shelved so steeply that they couldn't even wade out 2 or 3 yd, but for some reason they felt obliged to wade. The more I see of reservoir trout fishing, the more convinced I become that we would all be better off if nobody waded at all, not only financially but in terms of catches. The amount of trout food destroyed by wading anglers is enormous.

I have resolved to reduce the barbs on all the hooks I use, till I can get Geoff Bucknall's new microbarbs. I don't trust barbless hooks, but standard hooks have barbs that are too big, too deeply cut, and turned up too much. I am seldom broken by trout, but quite a few come off the hook; and when that happens, nine times out of ten it's because the hook wasn't ever in over its barb.

Carbon rods don't stick hooks in as firmly as rods of glass or cane, simply because they're lighter. A hook with a tiny barb goes in more easily. So get the lead out, Geoffrey, and let's all have some of those! I hope there will be some with small straight eyes; why anyone should want turned-up or turned-down eyes, I can't understand. Does anyone

38

tie on flies with Turle knots, which are weak and unreliable, nowadays? I stopped using that knot when silkworm gut was replaced by nylon.

Talking of carbon rods, I've recently acquired a couple of match rods in this material. They call them match rods, but they'll do fine for general coarse fishing, other than carp, pike, barbel and big chub or tench in reedy or snaggy water. They'll also do for dapping for trout from a drifting boat, where that's allowed. So there's another resolution – tie some dapping flies, like Daddy-long-legs, big Red Sedges and so on. But if I run true to previous form there will be at least three important things I ought to have done, but haven't done, by the opening day of the trout season of 1980.

Cooking Your Trout

Next to catching the fish, the most important thing in making a trout into a delicious meal is what happens between catching and cooking it. Don't put it in a plastic bag, or the waterproof compartment found in some fishing bags.

If you can fish close to your car, or from a boat, make or buy an insulated box into which you can put your fish immediately after it is caught and killed. The box must contain either blocks of ice in a secured plastic bag, or half a dozen freeze packs. Failing this, put the fish into a fishmonger's bass, in the shade, first wiping each fish dry. When you get your fish home, wash them thoroughly in cold, salted water with a half-cup of malted vinegar added, squeeze out any excreta from the anus and remove all the slime from the entire skin.

There is never any need to remove the scales before cooking a trout. Clean it by cutting along the underside from the anus up to the head (we prefer to cut off the head and tail) and take out all the innards, making sure to scrape out the dark reddish-brown matter that lies close to the backbone. Then wash it thoroughly.

We are talking here about good fish caught from rivers, lakes and reservoirs, weighing upwards of 1 lb, which have plenty of flavour on their own without need of special cooking disguises. Two excellent ways of cooking trout that we use most frequently are grilling and baking.

First, grilling, which is particularly suitable for fish up to about 1½ lb–2 lb at most. Either slice off two fillets, or remove head, tail and skeleton. A friendly fishmonger will show you how to bone it, especially if you give him one or two fish from your catch! However, a tip if you decide to try boning it yourself is that you cut the fillets by attacking the back of the fish. Whether boned or filleted, and if not boned open like a kipper by cutting with a very sharp knife down one side of the backbone, put the fish skin downwards on the grill pan. Sprinkle with salt and black pepper, smear with butter and grill for four to eight minutes according to size. That's all!

The other method is baking, that is suitable for all sizes of trout but best for bigger fish. Cut off the head and also the tail, to allow the fish to fit the cooking vessel, unless you like to keep the fish intact to glaze and decorate the trout for a buffet. Use a liquid consisting of one part malt vinegar or white wine to two parts water; a dessert-spoonful of salt per pint of liquid; a good teaspoonful of mixed pickling spice; and about 2 oz of butter which you put inside the fish. You want enough liquid to come about halfway up the fish. Don't be afraid of vinegar; you won't taste it when the fish is cooked. Vinegar is better than wine if there is any risk of a muddy flavour in your fish; otherwise, white wine is superior, though more expensive.

If your vessel hasn't a lid, cover it with kitchen foil. Put it in the oven, at 350°F (medium oven, Regulo 4) and let it cook for about ten minutes. Then gently turn the fish over in its liquid, and cook for another ten to 25 minutes, depending on the size of the fish and the type of vessel you are using. For six-pounders and above, 15 minutes to the pound is a guide. Baste occasionally.

To serve hot, when the fish is done, lift it out of the liquid and let it drain. You will tell when it is cooked by being able to insert a fork easily up to the backbone, and finding that with a blunt knife you can easily lift the skin. This should be peeled off, and then two slabs of flesh can be removed from each side of the skeleton, one above and one below the lateral line. Place these on a rectangular or oval hot dish, and serve with mustard sauce, or the sauce we describe to accompany cold trout.

To serve cold, leave the fish to drain and cool. Then the skin and flesh can be dealt with as mentioned above. This way the trout can be used as a starter, or a main course, placed on a dish and decorated with parsley, tomato slices and a little lettuce. A good sauce for cold trout is made up as follows: to half a cup of mayonnaise add two

40

teaspoonfuls of malt vinegar and two of tomato purée. Sprinkle with red pepper, or add a few drops of Tabasco sauce to taste, and thoroughly mix.

Suitable wines to drink with a good trout range from Liebfrau-milch through various Hocks and Moselles, to the drier French white wines like Pouilly-Fuissé or, if you like a very dry wine, Pouilly-Fumé. They should be served chilled, whether you eat your trout hot or cold.

It is generally supposed that the pinker the flesh of a trout, the better the flavour, but this is not always the case. What matters is that the trout is in good, firm condition. Some white-fleshed trout make excellent eating. It all depends on the water where the fish is caught and what the fish has been feeding on. In fact it is impossible to tell from the appearance of the fish what it will taste like; rather like a piece of meat it is not until you start to eat it! We suggest to friends that they have a tin of ham handy, just in case.

Grayling can be cooked in exactly the same way, but although it is not essential, it is certainly preferable to scale them before cooking, since the scales are hard and sharp edged and must not be allowed to find their way onto your or your guest's plate.

Incidentally, be very careful not to over-cook your trout as it will make the flesh dry, instead of being succulent, juicy and delicious.

The Evening Rise

The activity among most kinds of fish that begins in the evening – the trout-fisher's 'evening rise' – is a well-known phenomenon to all fresh-water anglers and, for all I know, it may apply to sea fish as well.

Various theories have been put forward to account for it, including cooling water after a warm day, the hatching at lower light levels of different insects, and, in still waters, the upward migration of zooplankton, mostly daphnia, as the light fades.

A more attractive theory, to my mind, is that involving refraction angles. A light ray that strikes the surface of calm water at an angle of about ten degrees or less is totally reflected; none penetrates the surface at all. This angle is not exact, since it is slightly different for different light colours, but is sufficient for our purpose to say 'about ten degrees'.

This means that on a clear day, as soon as the sun makes an angle of ten degrees or less to the water's surface, there is a very sharp reduction in subsurface illumination, specially if the surface is calm, as is very often the case at that time of day, when any breeze blowing is likely to drop.

In these circumstances, any creature above the surface of the water will find it almost impossible to see below it. Fish are therefore relatively safe from terrestrial and avian predators, and may be expected to know this instinctively, and to forage actively for food.

The lower light level beneath the surface may also reduce the danger from some subsurface predators; certainly, pike and perch do relatively little feeding when the sun is below the critical ten-degree angle, though eels, which rely more on scent than light, become more active then.

I do not suggest that the shut-off of subsurface light gives fish total immunity from predation; there is reason to believe that herons, for example, can fish fairly successfully at night, but perhaps they do so only when the vigilance of those who look after fish farms and fisheries have made it too dangerous for them to fish in the daytime.

Whatever the reason, many fish do commence to feed in the evening. While this provides the coarse-fish angler with excellent opportunities of which he usually takes advantage, it often leads to frustration for the fly-fisher, who finds trout rising in numbers and with abandon, but cannot persuade any of them to accept his artificial fly.

His inability to do so is usually ascribed to incorrect choice of pattern, and no doubt that may often be the case.

However, as Clarke and Goddard have shown in their book *The Trout and the Fly*, anything floating on the surface appears very prominently to fish when the angle of the light to the surface is small — below ten degrees — while artificial flies appear differently from how they look with higher light angles.

A remarkable thing about nearly all the books about dry-fly fishing, whether ancient or modern, is their omission of any advice about whether the leader should sink or float, yet this is a question frequently asked by novices. In the days of silkworm gut, which had to be well soaked before use, the leader must have sunk a little, unless greased, and we can infer from G.E.M. Skues's famous 'dry-fly oil tip' that a sunken leader was usually used, the 'oil tip' being advice to oil or grease part of the leader to make it float in order to detect that a sunk fly or nymph had been taken.

Nylon, however, often floats, and in dry-fly fishing, it is common for some of whatever waterproofing substance has been used on the fly to be transferred to the leader by one means or another, and this will ensure that it floats.

A floating leader is liable to alarm trout in any conditions, particularly in sunshine and most of all when that sunshine is striking the water at a low angle. With the aid of a glass-bottomed basin and a movable artificial light source, I have been able to confirm this. It therefore seems likely that, at least in many cases, refusal by the trout to take an artificial fly during the evening rise may be due to failure to ensure that the leader sinks directly it falls on the water.

It is not difficult to make it do so; proprietary preparations are available, or the angler can mix equal parts of glycerine and neat washing-up detergent liquid, and then stir in enough fuller's earth to make a stiff enough ball to be handled without its sticking to the fingers. Such a ball, kept in a really airtight container and moistened with water occasionally, will last for several seasons of fishing. It is superior to soap, since the minute trace of fuller's earth left on the leader reduces its tendency to flash in the air in casting.

There are, of course, other factors that may combine to make an evening rise frustrating. If the angler is on the western side of the water he will cast a very long shadow when the sun is low. This shadow need not fall upon the fish he is trying to catch; it can alarm other fish and produce a chain reaction that panics all the fish for several hundred yards.

If on the other hand the angler is on the eastern side, he will be brightly illuminated, because he will receive not only the direct rays of a low sun, but also the total reflection of these rays from the water's surface. Unless his clothing blends very well with the background, his movements will be readily seen by many of the fish, when a chain reaction of panic is again likely. In particular, a white fly-line being false-cast is very likely to scare fish, even at a distance beyond that at which they can see the angler.

One may sum up by saying that while, in the fading light of evening, the angler may be tempted to assume that the trout cannot see him so well, the reverse is actually the case, and that his need for

43

care in moving and in choosing his position is greater than at any other time of day or night.

Coming Short

'They're coming short today!'

How often do we hear this said, or perhaps say it ourselves, especially in wet-fly fishing? One feels a sharp pluck, then nothing. Often, a spell of fishing will bring a series of these exasperating plucks, with few or no fish hooked.

There can be more than one cause of this kind of thing. One of them is that the trout actually *are* 'coming short'; that is, they are not taking the fly properly. This kind of behaviour is by no means confined to trout; it can be observed at times in many other species. Carp, tench, bream and chub often pick up a bait very delicately between their lips and make off with it, usually rapidly, whereupon the angler strikes fruitlessly. Pike, too, will sometimes take a live or dead fish, shake it, and drop it.

This behaviour can sometimes be seen with baits that are not attached to a hook and line, and it is certain that fish do at times pick up food that they do not mean to eat. When trout are behaving so, there is very little that the angler can do about it, because it seems that the behaviour is extended to all forms of food while it persists. A change of fly is very unlikely to result in the fish taking more positively, though there may be a possibility that an increase in the likelihood of a short riser being hooked can be effected in some circumstances, perhaps by using a multi-hooked fly or one dressed short on a long hook-shank. Such expedients seldom provide anything like a full answer to the problem, however, and many anglers will remember days when even three-hooked lures were subject to repeated plucks without a fish being hooked.

It is important to distinguish genuine cases of the fish coming short from fish that are missed for other reasons that the angler can cure.

A very common cause of an angler complaining that fish are coming short is when the trout takes a fly and immediately comes up against the resistance of a stiff rod-top. The fairly powerful rods used in reservoir fly-fishing cause many a trout to eject the fly before the angler can strike, especially when the retrieve is carried out with the rod held approximately horizontal and pointing straight at the fly. This is in fact the most common position in which one sees rods being held. It is not enough of a handicap to encourage its abandonment, because some trout hook themselves, and some provoke a quick enough reaction through the angler's hand that is drawing line which, combined with a raising of the rod, results in their being hooked. Many, however, fail to be hooked because they eject the fly in time.

Far more would be hooked if the rod were held up more, leaving a considerable sag in the line between the rod-tip and the water. It is quite surprising how long trout will hang on to an artificial fly, if they feel no resistance from the line. They will sometimes swim ten yards or more, towing a floating line along the surface.

Lines, of course, offer their own resistance, and a trout moving directly towards the angler will feel it least. Surprisingly, it will also feel relatively little if it moves directly away from him, if his rod-tip is held fairly high. It feels most when it is moving approximately at right angles to a line joining angler and fly, because then some of the heavy line is pulled sideways. This means there is a strong case for using a fly-line that is no thicker than is needed to obtain sufficient casting range, and of course a floating line offers far less resistance than a sunken one.

The perennial debate about the importance of imitation and presentation sometimes obscures clear thinking. The debate is of course rather sterile if one realises that presentation is nothing more than one aspect of imitation, but it should also be realised that a trout does not necessarily choose between taking or rejecting a fly. He may take it suspiciously because it fails to imitate his natural food sufficiently accurately, either in movement or appearance, or both.

This means that, although it is usually fruitless to change the fly when trout are coming short in their pattern of behaviour, it may prove profitable when fish are simply being felt and missed, because the fault may be due to partial failure in some aspect of imitation, and not to true coming short at all.

Another possible cause of apparent coming short is a badly designed fly or lure, as for example one in which the hook-point is masked by a stiff hackle, or where the gape is altogether insufficient in relation to the bulk of the dressing. Some flies, too, have a good deal of dressing trailing far behind the bend of the hook, or the last hook in a tandem lure. These are all points to be watched, or the proportion of hookings to offers will be reduced.

There is also the question of distance. Although there is a compensating factor, it is clearly more difficult to hook a trout at 40 yd than it is at 20. The compensating factor is the reduced likelihood of the fish feeling the rod-top at long range, but the compensation is not sufficient to load the scales in favour of the angler who is fishing at extreme range; they remain tipped the other way, except when we come to very short ranges. Then, the rod-top is felt so soon and so definitely that the angler cannot help a high proportion of misses. In stillwater fly-fishing, it pays when fishing very near water to do it from the bank with a line of moderate length, rather than to wade out and retrieve down to a very short line.

Regardless of all these considerations, easy hook penetration cannot do other than favour the angler, yet it is amazing how few anglers pay attention to the kind of hooks on which the flies are dressed, or will take the trouble to carry a small stone with which they can ensure that every fly they fish has a really keen point.

PART TWO
Flies

Fly-Tying

F ollowing some magazine articles of mine about new fly patterns for stillwater trout fishing, quite a number of readers who wrote for information about these dressings and received sample flies have followed up with requests for details of my tying techniques.

Let me say at once that I am not a professional fly-tyer, and make no pretence even of being an expert amateur; but I've been tying flies for a very long time and there may be a few points in my ways of doing things that would interest others. I shall therefore pick out such points as my friends tell me are unorthodox.

First of all, I never use wax. I coat the hook shank with cellulose varnish, quick-drying, directly after setting the hook in the vice and testing it, and I begin the tying at once. Wax has always been a nuisance whenever I've tried it. If it is really sticky, it sticks to everything, including my fingers. If it isn't sticky enough, there's no advantage in using it. If it is used, it prevents cellulose from soaking in properly, and that is essential in many of the flies I tie because of the form of construction I adopt.

I am told professional fly-dressers find that the judicious use of waxes made to secret formulae speeds up their operations, provided the room in which they work is kept at exactly the right temperature. Some even scream in anguish if someone opens a window! As I am not tying flies against a clock, but am very concerned about durability, I prefer cellulose.

The reason for wanting a good soak-in of cellulose is that for the majority of wet flies I tie, the wings and throat hackles consist of bunches of fibre or hair lashed to the hook shank. There seems to me no point at all in setting wings carefully on a fly, whether rolled or made from slips cut from opposite wing feathers. In two or three casts, all you have is a bunch of fibres and you may just as well use that in the first place. I simply tear a bunch from a suitable feather and lash them down with the tying silk, or snip a bunch of hair fibres from a skin and tie them down in the same way. To keep them from moulting when fishing, the lashings need soaking with cellulose.

The same applies to throat hackles in wet flies. A wisp of cock-hackle fibres is torn from a hackle feather and tied in under the shank, below the wing roots. These methods make a neat fly with a good entry, that will stand up to any amount of long casting, and they are much quicker than the conventional methods.

An alternative to bunches of fibre or hair, that I use in some dressings, is hackle-points. These are used sloping well back in some wet-fly dressings, and nearly vertical in dry flies. They are tied in by the stalks in the usual way, but here again, a lashing well soaked in cellulose ensures they don't come adrift.

Hackle points seem to me much more satisfactory for dry-fly wings than slips of feather fibre. If a fairly opaque feather is wanted to imitate sub-imago ephemerids, a hen-hackle can be used. There are advantages in upwinged hackle-point dry-flies. They parachute down onto the water more gently, and they bring less water with them when lifted off. This is particularly true of mayfly imitations. The fashion nowadays, where mayflies are still found, is to use hackle imitations, but it isn't always easy to let them down gently on the water with the comparatively heavy leader points that are necessary to push these air-resisting flies into a wind.

The old-fashioned Mayflies with dyed mallard feathers for wings were bad hookers, being so stiff because of the ribs of the feathers, but broad cock-hackle wings are much more collapsible. They give an excellent parachute effect and still hook fish very well.

For imitations of nymphs and other underwater creatures I tend to use very soft feathers indeed. I am always being told that these feathers are useless when wet, a notion that arises from examining the soaked fly in the air.

In that condition, very soft feathers like water rail, water hen and ostrich look horribly bedraggled and the fly seems a shapeless lump; but lower it into a glass of clear water and the appearance is restored at once to approximately what it was when the fly was dry. There may be some darkening in colour, which must be allowed for in choosing the colours of the materials used in dressing the fly; but the thing certainly doesn't look bedraggled, and the softer the fibres are, the more realistically they move under water.

Centuries ago, Charles Cotton pointed out the importance of examining materials against the light. Even more important is to examine any fly or lure intended to be fished sunk, under water.

I prefer whenever possible to tie flies on ringed hooks. 'Ringed' is the trade term for a straight eye. I can see no advantage whatever in having eyes turned up or down; my flies are attached to the leader point by means of a tucked Half-Blood knot. The stresses of casting ensure that the fly alights on the water dead in line with the leader point, and this knot is much more reliable than the Turle and its variations.

Fluorescent Materials and Fly-tying

It must be some 20 years since fluorescent materials for fly-tying first became available. Since then they have been used extensively, but without very much logical thinking.

Until recently, it was believed that the fluorescent effect was lost at depths greater than a foot or two, owing to the attenuation by water of the ultra-violet light that is converted to light of a lower wavelength by the fluorescent material; but it now seems that this is not the case, and that even at considerable depths, fluorescent wools, silks and synthetic threads show enhanced colour compared to non-fluorescent equivalents.

In stillwater trout-fishing, and specially on reservoirs, it is clear that fluorescent materials in large lures do increase their effectiveness, and examples of its use include the Sweeney Todd, Mrs Palmer, Church Fry and Baby Doll. In all these the fluorescent material is used in some or all of the body, and except in the all-white Baby Doll, it involves therefore only a minor part of the pattern.

What is not very well known is the fact that a cut end of fluorescent thread produces enhanced fluorescence. When tying a fly with a fluorescent wool body, it helps, after the body is wound and the end secured, but before winding on ribbing, to rub the body lightly with sandpaper. The sanded wooden slips used for manicure are ideal for the job, giving the body a slightly fluffy or downy appearance.

Fluorescence has for a long time been considered inappropriate in imitative fly patterns by most anglers, but there are indications that it may after all have merits for these. Quite a long time ago, Pat Russell of Romsey produced a pattern for the Iron Blue with a body of dark heron herl, a dun hackle and tails, but with a turn of fluorescent magenta wool at the rear end of the body, and this has proved to be a most successful dry-fly. Later he invented a dressing for the Grannom, with a green fluorescent end to its body, and that too was a killer.

My most successful pattern for imitating various sedges, of which many species are predominantly reddish-brown, has a turn of arc chrome (yellowish-orange) fluorescent wool at the back end, and this pattern has, over the last ten years, been my most killing dry-fly on still waters, and extremely useful for both trout and grayling on rivers.

A few weeks ago, a contributor to *The Field* mentioned fly bodies made from mixed dubbings and I am quite sure that the future will see further valuable developments in this direction. Before the advent of really effective silicone-wax waterproofing liquids like Permaflote, water-absorbent dubbings were unsatisfactory for floating flies, but now we can use all sorts of wool, furs and synthetic materials without fear of waterlogging. One can even make cottonwool and blotting paper float all day with these proofing agents.

This makes the judicious incorporation of fluorescent wool in a dry-fly body quite easy. For example, the chestnut body of a female olive spinner can consist of brown silk dubbed with fine chestnut-coloured wool with which a very little vermilion fluorescent wool has been intimately mixed. A little arc chrome fluorescent wool can be mixed with a dull apricot-coloured wool to dub a body for a pale watery spinner. Experienced anglers will decide easily what may make suitable mixed wool dubbings for other common aquatic insects.

The use of fluorescent materials in imitative patterns is not confined to floaters. A few years ago, I discovered a larva, presumably that of some kind of midge, that lives in the blue-green algae which form on the bottom of clear lakes. Under the influence of increased water temperature, natural gases form in the bottom mud and cause lumps of the algae to rise to the surface. In hot weather this sometimes happens in such profusion that fishing is made difficult.

The larvae living in the algae do not care to be at the surface, and when their home ascends, they wriggle out and go back to the bottom. Trout intercept them avidly. They have green abdomens with sepia rear segments and sepia thoraces. I produced a very simple pattern to imitate these larvae: it has a short body, extending only halfway down the shank of a No 6 hook, of what is called phosphor-yellow fluorescent wool which in appearance is of a lime-green colour. When wet, it matches the green larva well, the exposed bronzed hook imitating the sepia front and rear. Simply to reduce the sinking rate, there is a grey partridge hackle at the head, two turns only.

This pattern, which even a novice fly-tyer can easily produce, is startlingly effective when green algae are rising to the surface. I have caught lots of trout with it, including seven between 10¼ and 13½ lb. Where very large trout are found, the knowledge that one is fishing with a relatively big and strong hook is comforting. Another pattern differs only from this in having a body of orange instead of phosphor-yellow wool; what it imitates I do not know, but it would seem that the trout do, since it is at times very successful.

The phosphor-yellow colour, in floss rather than wool, also has a use in imitating a small green and yellow corixa that is common in some waters. This is tied short on a No 10 hook; its body is of primrose floss, with a back of the phosphor-yellow floss tied over it in a similar way to an imitation of a fresh-water shrimp. A very sparse short pale buff hackle completes the dressing. Alternatively the back can consist of a strip of pale fluorescent green synthetic raffia; it looks nicer but is more easily destroyed by trout teeth. The whole dressing should occupy only half the length of the hook-shank; the fact that the hook is large in relation to the dressing makes the pattern a quick sinker.

One of the most popular patterns for lake, loch and reservoir is the Mallard and Claret, but despite its success in the hands of others, it never caught more than an odd fish for me, until I began mixing a little magenta fluorescent wool with the claret seal's fur body dubbing. Now it does much better, whether from real attraction or through my having more confidence in it, I cannot tell. I suspect, however, that many of the traditional lake patterns, the Teals, Grouses and Mallards, might benefit from a judicious admixture of fluorescent materials of appropriate colours.

To sum up, it would seem that fluorescent materials, specially wool that can be teased out and mixed with other dubbing materials, can help to increase the attraction of many artificial fly patterns, and perhaps lead to the invention of more effective new designs.

Different Ways of Tying Dry Flies

During the last hundred years, numbers of ingenious methods of tying dry flies have been invented and reinvented, and I have no doubt that as interest in trout fishing and amateur fly-tying continues to expand, most, if not all, of these methods will be reinvented over and over again in the future.

None of them has been shown to be superior to conventional tying methods for catching trout, and most of them have lesser or greater disadvantages.

One of the first of them was devised by R. B. Marston, for many years owner and editor of The *Fishing Gazette* in the 1880s. It was described in a book by the famous H. Cholmondeley-Pennell, entitled *Modern Developments in Fishing Tackle*. The idea was to dress dry flies upside down; the wings were on the same side of the hook shank as the bend and point, and Marston had hooks specially made, of a shape intended to increase the likelihood of the fly alighting point up.

Unlike the majority of innovators, however, Marston later wrote that after a full season's use of the flies, he was unable to find that they offered any advantage over conventional patterns.

In the 1960s, Dick Polest reinvented the 'upside-down' dry fly and, like Marston, had special hooks made. More recently, John Goddard and Brian Clarke have pursued the idea, combining the upside-down dressing with a parachute hackle. There is no evidence that would suggest that these flies are any more effective than the ordinary ones. It is true that they have accounted for some trout that refused normal flies, but this was on a water where most of the trout are returned alive after being caught, and are therefore suspicious of patterns on which they were previously taken. I have no doubt that different patterns, tied in the normal way, would have deceived these fish as well as the upside-down, parachute-hackled flies.

Some of the Clarke-Goddard flies are tied on what are known as Keel hooks, which I understand were invented by the same Dick Polest who pursued the upside-down idea. These are long-shanked hooks with two 45-degree bends in the shank, which bring the eye in line with the point. The object of this is to prevent the hook from catching on weeds, snags, twigs and so on, and in this the design is quite effective. It is also quite effective in preventing the hook from catching fish, since its angle of penetration is zero!

The same drawback was found in a special dry-fly hook invented by Alexander Wanless, whose writings in favour of the fixed-spool reel between 1930 and 1950 caused so much controversy. This hook had a bend in the middle of its shank which reduced the angle of penetration to a minus quantity. The object was to ensure that the fly alighted 'cocked', that is with its wings upright, since the centre of gravity was well below where it is with conventional hooks.

Wanless's flies always alighted correctly and cocked beautifully, but only rarely hooked fish which took them.

Yet another peculiar hook that appeared quite recently was the Yorkshire Flybody hook. This was intended to form a basis for flies with detached bodies; that is, bodies formed separately instead of on the hook shank. Such bodies were devised towards the end of the last century and were for some years quite popular, Victorian anglers, having discovered that if the bodies were made of soft latex, the flies caught fish quite well. Any stiff material in the body, however, made it difficult for trout to suck the fly in, a point that has been overlooked by the many who have resurrected the detached body idea in later years.

The Yorkshire Flybody hook has a metal extrusion above the shank which is completely rigid, making flies dressed on it difficult for fish to take, and if that were not enough, the point is directly under the eye, so that the angle of penetration, in the original hooks, was 90 degrees, making hooking a fish almost impossible. Later versions had the point angled upwards towards the eye, so that if trout did succeed in taking the fly despite the rigid detached body, the possibility of hooking it existed; but flies tied on these hooks remained far less effective for catching trout than ordinary hooks.

I mentioned that the Clarke-Goddard upside-down flies incorporated parachute hackles, which, as far as I can trace, were introduced in the late 1920s or early 1930s, and flies incorporating them were retailed by Alex Martin Ltd of Glasgow, who had special hooks made incorporating a tiny stub of metal at right angles to the back of the shank, around which the hackle was wound. This placed most of the hackle-fibres more or less parallel to the surface of the water, so that the fly was better supported in the surface film than it would be by conventional hackles, many of whose fibres were – and are – approximately vertical and thus prone to penetrate the surface film easily, especially with very stiff cock-hackles.

Stiff cock-hackles were preferred in the early days of dry-fly fishing, before the advent of waterproofing agents, because they absorbed very little water and were easily dried by false casting. The belief that dry flies need stiff cock-hackles was so firmly established at that time that it has never been abandoned, and hardly ever questioned. So firmly is it held that the words 'stiff' and 'good' have become synonymous, and the translucent, sparkling appearance of such hackles is generally held to be advantageous, despite the very obvious fact that very few of the insects we imitate with dry flies are anything but rather dull-coloured creatures with a matt finish to bodies, wings and legs.

The truth is that softer hackles support dry flies better than stiff ones, because the soft fibres bend when they touch the surface. These softer hackles also make the flies easier to suck in by the fish, and now that we have silicone-wax dip-in waterproofing liquids, there is no problem of the fibres becoming waterlogged. Flies tied with these softer hackles float as well as those with parachute hackles and are very much easier to tie.

Another regularly reinvented idea is the reversed dry fly, in which the wings and hackle are placed at the beginning of the hook bend and the tails extend forwards over the eye. Such flies are rather awkward to tie, and it is difficult to attach them to the leader-point without involving the tail-fibres in the knot, but they seem to have no other disadvantages, even if they catch no more fish.

At this point, it should be said that the object of these reversed flies, and of the upside-down patterns, seems to be mainly to prevent the fish from seeing the bend, point and barb of the hook. It is true that when one compares an artificial fly with a real one, the hook bend, barb and point look very obtrusive indeed, and while there are other rather obvious differences between real and artificial, the hook is the most arresting.

The fact is, however, that fish are not in the least concerned at the appearance of the hook. If they were, we should never catch any on conventional flies of any sort, including some wet patterns in which not only the point, barb and bend are exposed, but a good deal of the shank as well. Consequently, expedients to conceal the hook are wasted ingenuity, though no doubt they will continue to be invented and reinvented.

One other device for lifting – or retaining – dry flies higher above the water's surface, and thus helping to conceal the hook, was the so-called fore-and-aft system. It was popularised by Horace Brown of the Piscatorial Society 50 or 60 years ago, and consisted of a body wound along the shank, with a hackle wound behind the eye and another at the rear of the body, at the start of the bend. Mainly used in mayfly imitations, it was nearly as successful as ordinary patterns, though somewhat awkward to tie, and enjoyed quite a vogue for some years.

Itchen – Sunset over the chalk stream, between Chilland and Faston.

Lambourn – Netting a sizeable brown trout from the chalk stream.

River Test – Trout fishing on a windy day above Romsey, Hants.

Chalk stream charm on the River Wylye, Wilts., where brown trout rise freely.

River Test – a big mayfly hatch coming off the water as a fish is being played on Greatbridge water.

Action with a lively brown trout on the River Test.

The author with three fish caught from Damerham Lakes in Hampshire – the best weighed in at 5lb 6oz, caught on a floating mayfly.

Damerham Trout Lakes 1973 – the trout were rising on Mayfly Lake as the author casts near the trees.

Opposite top: Two Lakes – Romsey. A brace of brown trout which weighed just under 5lb.

Opposite bottom: The author.

Casting a long line into the wind – the author at Grafham Water.

No shortage of fly-patterns! This picture shows only half of the contents of the stillwater fly-box, which is double-hinged.

The author displays the results of his fly-tying skills.

Two early season rainbows, both over 2lb and in fine condition, caught on an insect-imitating pattern.

Too many angling books!

Playing a fighting trout on the Test near Stockbridge.

Playing a 4lb trout on Latimer Park Lakes.

Horizontal casting is often needed. Here the angler must avoid the branches at top right.

The author.

Anton – Evening rise.

The extra hackle, however, made it more difficult for trout feeding half-heartedly to suck in, specially when it was dressed with the stiffest available hackles, which it usually was, and one seldom sees fore-and-aft dry flies now. The idea still has its uses for sunk flies intended to be fished right at the bottom of lakes and reservoirs, where the hackles keep the point of the hook above the silkweed or other lake-bed rubbish.

From time to time, materials such as celluloid, cellophane and other kinds of synthetic film have been tried for dry-fly wings, specially in imitating spent spinners. They look very realistic, but the aerodynamic qualities of all that I ever tried were conspicuously lacking; I remember one range of patterns that not only made a noise like a chorus of demented grasshoppers when being false-cast, but which spun like aircraft propellers, twisting up the leader into devastating kinks. A recent innovation involves cellophane wings for small spinners, perforated all over with a pin. Seen from below the surface, these wings are very realistic indeed, but unfortunately they fold backwards in casting and become trapped under the bend of the hook.

It therefore seems sad but true that a century of ingenuity in the physical design of dry flies has failed to produce any advantages whatever for catching trout. There have been advances in materials and in the understanding of what features are necessary in an artificial fly to make it attractive to trout; but otherwise, we are where we were in the 1880s.

They caught trout as successfully then as we do now.

Mayflies

In his *Dictionary of Trout Flies*, the late Major A. Courtney Williams said that the mayfly had given rise to more artificial patterns than any other insect, and there can be no doubt that he was right. Since the time of Dame Juliana Berners in the fifteenth century, anglers have been trying to produce better mayflies, and it is interesting to consider why these insects should have stimulated the production of so many different patterns, since the season in which they appear is relatively short, whichever of the three species we consider. There are few rivers or lakes where the hatch goes on for more than about three weeks, though sometimes a small sprinkling of the fly appears well before, or long after, the normal mayfly period. Usually, when it does, the trout ignore it.

Part of the proliferation of patterns may stem from the fact that once the trout start taking mayfly freely, fish of all sizes join in the feast, and more fishing takes place than usual. Fish are often caught and released as undersized, or because anglers set themselves higher standards of size in this period. Numbers of fish are also pricked, or hooked and lost; and the overall effect is to produce a higher proportion of fish that have learned to recognise features in the artificial fly that they identify as danger signals.

It is therefore quite common, after the mayfly season is several days old, to come across fish that refuse popular patterns of artificial mayfly, while they continue to feed on the natural insects. Some of these fish are large and thus provide the angler with considerable incentive to try different patterns or even to devise new ones.

There is no doubt that one sharp lesson is sufficient to teach a trout to avoid a particular dressing, but that fish will accept another pattern that imitates the same insect, but in a different way. I used to fish a water that had a splendid mayfly season, but where we who fished it returned nearly all the trout we caught. Some of these fish had, by the end of the mayfly season, learned to avoid as many as four mayfly patterns.

The very nature of some artificial mayflies enhances their educational value to the trout. Wings with stiff ribs, like the popular duck feathers, and detached bodies, make hooking less likely and pricking more so. In addition, there is variation in the state of the natural insect due to weather; in mayfly time, short but heavy showers of rain often occur, which beat the hatching fly into the surface film. When that happens, a high-floating artificial looks suspicious to the fish. Yet more proliferation is encouraged by the fact that female mayflies are nearly twice as big as the males, and we find, now and then, a trout that is concentrating on eating one or the other.

Over very many years of trying to invent better mayflies, I have come more and more to avoid stiff-ribbed wings. Whole-feather wings made from poultry hackle-points are more flexible than the popular duck feathers, but a bunch of fibres stripped from the hackle stalk and tied in as a simple bunch are more flexible still, whether tied

58

upright to imitate the newly hatched fly, or horizontal to imitate the spent insect. It is especially important to avoid any stiff element in the latter, since it is seldom taken with the wide-open mouth with which the trout accept the freshly hatched fly with its upright wings. Since the spent fly should lie flat on the water's surface, it seems pointless to provide it with numerous turns of stiff cock-hackle as well as wings. The real insect has but six legs, and a single turn of any soft black or dark brown feather is sufficient hackling.

The imitation of the fresh fly can be tied with or without wings; if the latter is made with soft wing material, I prefer it as a first offering; if an educated fish refuses it, I have a choice of several hackle patterns to offer. These have two or even three hackles: a speckled feather like grey partridge or duck, sometimes dyed pale sea-green; a cock-hackle, natural red or dyed sea-green; and sometimes short, dark, soft hackle just behind the hook eye. This allows several feather combinations, each having at least a speckled and a non-speckled hackle, one of which is greenish, combined.

If these hackle patterns are also refused, there is yet another, in which, in addition to the other hackles, there is a third, a cock-hackle dyed hot orange. The efficacy of this addition in catching cunning trout was discovered a very long time ago, and was incorporated originally, as far as I can discover, in an Irish pattern called Goulden's Favourite. This addition of an orange hackle has often secured me a difficult fish, especially on heavily fished rivers, and it is equally applicable to imitations of the spent mayfly.

Mayfly bodies have always challenged ingenuity, and various materials have been tried, including raffia, cork, straw, Raffene, feather fibre, floss silk, cellulite and expanded polyethylene. The last, which is used largely as a packing material, is buoyant and has a degree of translucence as well as being very durable, but professional fly-dressers seem not to care for it, probably because in order to match the colour of the natural, it needs a coat of buff varnish. Recently, I have been using lightly dyed feather fibre from white turkey tail feathers, suitably ribbed; this fibre is stronger than that found on swan secondary wing feathers.

Before the modern dip-in waterproofing liquids became available, feather fibre bodies quickly became soaked and sank, but there is no such problem now, and the diffraction produced by the furry fibres gives an excellent illusion of translucence which, in many conditions of light, seems to make the patterns so tied appreciably more attractive than those with bodies of opaque material such as raffia, cork or floss.

For some curious reason, it has been fashionable for a century to tie artificial mayflies smaller than the real insects, size 12 hooks being usual. There is not the least evidence to suggest that trout prefer undersized insects; if anything, the reverse is the case. My dressings for female mayflies are tied on No 8 long-shank hooks; only the males are tied on No 12s and even those have long shanks, too. The large flies on the No 8s do, however, need a fairly stout leader point, especially in adverse winds, and I seldom use one finer than 6-lb b.s. The trout seem not to object to this; I have no reason to think, when my fly is refused, that a finer point would have made it acceptable. A change of pattern on the same point usually produces the desired result.

The mayfly season has often been called 'the duffer's fortnight', a misnomer if there ever was one, since the fly usually lasts for three weeks and on a water fished regularly by capable anglers, duffers are not conspicuously successful. It is, however, an interesting facet of trout fishing and often enables outsize fish to be sought, if not always caught.

Mayfly Nymphs

One of the most puzzling things about the literature of fly-fishing and fly-dressing is the manner in which it deals with, or more often fails to deal with, the nymph of our largest ephemerid species, the mayfly.

Many writers ignore this nymph altogether; others describe patterns alleged to imitate it that could never have been devised by anyone who had looked at the real insect.

Col. E.W. Harding, author of that famous book *The Flyfisher and the Trout's Point of View*, so often quoted since its publication in 1931, wrote: 'The most difficult of all the nymphs to represent adequately is that of the Mayfly', and he goes on to say, 'There is no doubt that a successful Mayfly nymph would add greatly to the pleasure of the Mayfly hatch.'

His own pattern, about whose success or failure he had nothing whatever to say, had a body consisting of 'a darkish buff mixture of natural wool, hare's ear and seal's fur' and his coloured illustration shows, indeed, quite a dark colour, a sort of dull chestnut, ribbed with a chocolate herl and gold wire. It is, in fact, typical of the various mayfly nymph dressings that have been described over the last 60 or 70 years, almost all of them comparatively dark in colour, which ranges from olive to brown.

Having dug my first mayfly nymphs from the silt at the bottom of a chalk stream some 50 years ago, and having examined several thousands at intervals since, I cannot understand why anyone should suppose that the creature is dark in colour. Its basic colour is in fact a sort of off-white or ivory colour, resembling that of a typical buff envelope but much paler. There are darker brown markings and the wing-cases and legs are brownish, but the animal is predominantly pale in colour, far, far paler than any of the dressings that have been devised, down the years, to imitate it.

There are three species of mayfly, *Ephemera vulgata*, *Ephemera lincata* and *Ephemera danica*. The nymphs of the first two are fractionally darker than those of the last but the difference is very slight and insufficient to justify tying more than one imitation.

Apart from the colour, perhaps the most striking feature of a mayfly nymph, looked at when alive and in the water, is the row of ciliae, the whiskery projections along each side of the abdomen. They are in constant and arresting motion, which takes the form of waves moving along the length of the insect's body, rather like the leg motion of a centipede, though they are not used for walking.

The mayfly nymph is, of course, much bigger than most other ephemerid nymphs, except for those of the uncommon species *siphlonurus*, which trout do not seem to like, but despite the size difference, the appearance and mobility of those ciliae are so very striking that I am sure that they constitute an important recognition feature.

When the nymph is seen against the light, its appearance becomes even more spectacular; it takes the form of two lines of shimmering brilliant light running down each side of the abdomen of the insect; and I am absolutely convinced that any artificial mayfly nymph on which the effect of these ciliae is not suggested must be inferior. Indeed I would go so far as to say that the limited success of most of the patterns extant is probably due to the omission of this feature.

Fortunately, it is not very difficult to suggest the ciliae. If the abdomen of the artificial is made from soft, very pale buff or yellowish wool, fairly closely ribbed with brown silk, tufts of wool can be pricked out from between adjacent turns of ribbing on each side. These tufts are then clipped to equal lengths, and the job is done.

Tails, legs and wing cases may be made of cock-pheasant tail-fibres. A nearer approximation to the pattern of markings in the real insect may be made by winding two bands of touching turns of the ribbing, near the rear end of the nymph.

To obtain the best results from these artificial nymphs, it is necessary to carry two versions, one heavily leaded and one un-leaded. The leaded version, tied on a No 8 long-shank hook, needs about six layers of wine-bottle lead foil bound firmly to the shank, under the dressing. Each strip of foil is shorter and wider than its predecessor, giving a cigar-shaped underbelly, which if biased to-wards the back of the hook shank causes the nymph to fish hook point upwards and thus avoid catching weed or bottom debris. The non-leaded version has a simple underbelly of pale orange floss, otherwise the dressing is the same.

This unleaded pattern is for use when mayflies are hatching, but the trout are taking the nymph just before or just as it reaches the surface, and are ignoring the hatched fly. It is fished just like a dry fly except that it comes down the current a little way below the surface. To prevent the floss underbody from becoming waterlogged, the nymph can be dipped in waterproofing fluid.

This version is also useful when one finds trout taking the winged fly but refusing the winged artificial. Such a fish will often take the artificial nymph just under the surface.

Early in the mayfly season, before the trout begin eating the hatched flies, the natural nymphs are active near the river-bed, making forays from their burrows in the silt. Trout are then found eating the nymphs at the bottom and it is then that the leaded artificial is required.

In water of modest depth it can be fished like the smaller nymph patterns, but in deeper water, or in a strong current, it is necessary to cast across the stream, laying the line on the surface in an upstream curve, which may be done by casting with the rod nearly horizontal. It is of course easier in an upstream wind. If the curve is insufficient, it can be increased by means of an upstream mend of the sort used in greased-line salmon-fishing.

The upstream curve in the floating line allows the nymph to sink unhindered until the current changes this curve into a downstream one, at which point the nymph is pulled upwards and is usually taken. The take is signalled by the end of the floating line stopping or being pulled down; all the angler need then do is tighten, when the fish will almost always be hooked firmly in the scissors.

Presumably because, although mayflies hatch mainly during a period of three weeks, there are always nymphs in the river, the killing powers of the artificial are not by any means confined to the period of the mayfly hatches. The leaded mayfly nymph, especially, will catch bottom-feeding trout at any time of the fishing season. It even catches them in waters where no natural mayflies are present in any form or at any time. One can only assume that trout have inherited instincts that enable them to recognise edible insects and other potential food organisms that they have never previously seen.

Chalk-stream Patterns

Since I wrote about the dearth of ephemerid flies on the chalk-streams, by comparison with fifty years ago, a surprisingly large number of people have written to ask me about suitable sunk patterns for catching trout that live mainly upon what they can find on or near the river-bed.

It must not be supposed that because we seldom see big hatches of ephemerids nowadays, these species have altogether disappeared. What seems to have happened is that there are fewer of all kinds, so that it is rare for enough to hatch simultaneously to induce a general rise. There are still nymphs in the river and trout still eat them. Consequently, imitations of nymphs are still very useful. Perhaps Frank Sawyer's Pheasant-tail nymph is the favourite where nymph-fishing is allowed; it certainly catches a lot of trout, and there are examples in my fly box.

Despite its proved effectiveness, I more often use an Olive nymph, made from dyed fibres from the tail of an albino cock pheasant. No other feather fibre is so strong as pheasant tail; though dyed swan feather fibre makes a nymph that is equally attractive to the trout, it is more prone to be cut by their teeth.

My nymphs are weighted with strips of lead foil saved from wine bottles, laid longitudinally along the back of the hook shank as the first operation in the dressing. Depending on the depth and current speed, I select a nymph that has one, two or three layers of the foil under its dressing, or none at all for shallow water. Nymphs are tied in three shades of olive – very light, medium and dark – in sizes 14 and 16.

Very often trout are seen feeding upon shrimps which seem to be much more numerous in chalk-streams nowadays, perhaps a sinister indication of the presence of more organic matter in the water. In the middle and lower Avon, the massive infestation of coarse fish with the hookworm *Pomporhynchus laevis*, to which the fresh-water shrimp is the intermediate host, may well be due to an increase in decaying organic matter from unknown sources. At any rate, the artificial shrimp is a good subsurface pattern, and it is made, as with the fast-sinking nymph imitations, by binding successive strips of lead foil, each a little shorter and wider than its predecessor, onto the back of the hook shank. For the shrimp, about five layers for a No 12 hook and seven layers for a No 10 is about right.

After binding down the lead, a big ginger cock-hackle is tied in at the rear end. The silk is dubbed with light olive wool and wound to just behind the eye, after which the hackle is wound on in open spirals, like the body of a Palmer fly, and secured.

All that then remains is to remove the fibres that project from the back and sides, and clip the rest to a length fractionally greater than the gape of the hook, after which the back is given successive coats of clear varnish until it is smooth and shiny.

This artificial shrimp not only swims upside-down like a real one but, because it fishes hook point upwards, it does not catch in the bottom and seldom in weed.

A somewhat similar pattern, which I devised for catching grayling, is called the Mead Mill Special. It has three layers of lead foil under the dressing, and the body consists of a mixture of three parts grass-green wool intimately mixed with one part lime-green d.r.f. wool, dubbed on olive silk and ribbed with fine gold thread. A bunch of speckled turkey-tail feather fibres is tied in at the rear end, brought forward over the body, and tied in behind the eye, to make a continuous back from stem to stern. Two of the fibres from this feather fibre are stroked back and secured by the tying silk, being cut off level with the hook bend; the rest are cut off and the head is finished in the usual way. The body dubbing is pricked out between the turns of ribbing. Sizes 10, 12 and 14 are all useful; the bigger ones go deeper.

Both this pattern and the shrimp are very good for both trout and grayling. They can be fished just like an upstream nymph, as described so well by Frank Sawyer, or they can be cast square across the current, the floating line being given an upstream mend to allow them adequate sinking time.

When in the past I have explained this technique, some people have raised their eyebrows, commenting that it deviates from upstream fishing. Naturally, one must abide by such rules as apply to the water one is fishing, but I must confess that I am impatient with alleged canons of sportsmanship that lack any logical basis.

Stewart advocated upstream wet fly because he considered it more effective, not because he regarded it as more ethical. There ensued a hot debate among the leading anglers of his time, which seems to have crystallised into the notion that it is immoral to cast in any direction other than upstream.

When rivers depended for their stocks upon natural breeding, and trout were present in a very wide range of sizes, down-and-across wet-fly fishing by an angler moving down a pace or two between casts and covering all the water as is usual on rain-fed rivers, was inappropriate to chalk streams. It caught or pricked many under-sized trout. But that is very different to casting a single fly across, or even down, to cover a selected fish whose size has been ascertained, especially now that stocking policies have made undersized fish relatively rare.

Surely matters have reached a pretty pass when, as has happened, committee meetings have spent time debating the question of what upstream fishing really is, arising from an instance of an angler who cast up the current of a back-eddy that ran opposite to the main flow of the river!

Bearing in mind that a trout is better able to see an angler opposite to or above him, it seems to me that provided the fish has been identified as of takeable size, it is quite ridiculous to argue that ethics are involved in the relative positions of man and trout in relation to the direction of the current.

Perhaps a few words about choice of pattern in relation to current speed and depth may be useful. One wishes to avoid letting the fish see the fly-line. Having spotted a good fish, it is essential to drop one's nymph or shrimp ahead of him, by a distance that ensures it sinking to his level before it reaches him. The deeper and faster the water, the farther upstream any given pattern will need to be cast to ensure this.

If the distance involved is too great, fly-line will fall too near the trout and scare him. The remedy is to use a more heavily leaded pattern, which is why I carry nymphs with different amounts of lead built in, as well as shrimps and Mead Mill Specials in different sizes – the bigger they are, the faster they sink.

It is also undesirable to drop the nymph or shrimp too close to the fish; one therefore avoids using a heavy pattern for fish in shallow water or slow currents. A lighter one will get down to such fish if it is cast a few feet above them.

From this, I hope, it will be realised that fishing sunk patterns involves not only accurate casting and manipulation but also a judicious choice of pattern. The use of sunk flies is no substitute for skill, judgement and keen observation, but it does enable one to catch some fish when dry-fly fishing would be useless.

Flies for the Test

When I fished the Test in my late teens and early twenties, the quantity and diversity of fly greatly exceeded what I see on the stretches that I fish nowadays. Recently I was reminded of this by reading an article in *The Field*.

It is now common to spend a day during which no hatch of fly appears, and most of the visible trout appear to be eating shrimps, small snails and other subaqueous organisms, a diet that autopsies often confirm. When a good old-fashioned hatch of fly provokes a fairly general rise, it often turns out to be one of pale wateries. As this insect, or group of insects, persists through October and is eaten by grayling, its imitation is of greater value than ever before, and it is surprising to find relatively little attention paid to it by fly-tyers past and present. It seems never to have commanded such interest as the olives, the iron blues and the blue-winged olive, which together with their female spinners, have been models for a large number of different artificial patterns.

Some years ago, with grayling mainly in mind, I devised a pattern for the sub-imago that has not only caught many grayling but also good numbers of trout. It is dressed on a No 16 hook as follows:

Silk, primrose
Whisks and hackle, cream cock
Dubbing, either two slips of palest starling, or a single vertical
    tuft of pale dun cock-hackle fibres
Body, swan secondary feather fibre dyed a very pale greyish-
    green

Three or four turns of the tying silk are exposed at the rear of the body and given a touch of clear varnish, which causes them to assume an amber shade, as does the whip finish at the head if similarly treated.

Before she left for the USA – she may soon return – Miss Jacqueline Wakeford of Romsey used to tie this little fly to perfection. Apart from her great skill, she succeeded in dyeing the body material in exactly the right colour and shade; regrettably, some other tyers made it grass-green. The tint should be so slight that it needs a second glance to see that the body of the fly is not in fact white, and if the correct shade is not obtained, it is better to use a plain white feather fibre than one which is excessively green. A swan feather that has been in the river for a week or two before being fished out is a very acceptable substitute.

More recently I have given some attention to the female spinner, for which the most popular imitation, I understand, is Lunn's Yellow Boy. That succeeds at times but less often than it should, which may be due either to lack of translucence in the body or to its having the conventional wound hackle, which causes it to sit too high on the water if it is waterproofed. Dabchick refers to his having fished his small-hackle Olive quill unoiled so that it floated low in the surface film, but to my mind that is not a very satisfactory practice, because it permits too few casts before the fly sinks. I cannot suggest any alternative for hackled or upwinged patterns intended to imitate the dun stage, but to imitate the spinner the problem is readily solved – by omitting the hackle and making the horizontal wings from bunches, either of cock-hackle fibres or some suitable fur.

The dressing for the female pale watery spinner is really very simple:

Silk, medium brown
Body, swan secondary feather fibre dyed pale orange-yellow,
    tinged light brown

67

Wings and whisks, pale dun cock-hackle fibres
Hook, size 16

The bunch of hackle fibres is tied in first with its points projecting beyond the eye. The butts are then cut off slantwise and the silk carried on down the shank, tying in eight to ten hackle fibres for the whisks. The silk is then wound back for about three exposed turns and the body herl tied in. Continue the silk back to the hackle bunch which is divided and spread flat by a figure-of-eight binding. Wind on the body material and double it at the wing roots to imitate the thicker thorax of the natural insect. Tie down and cut off the ends and whip-finish.

I should add that with all flies having feather-fibre bodies, it helps to varnish the turns of silk over which the fibre is to be wound and then wind it while the varnish is wet. This glues it down and prevents it from unwinding if cut by trout teeth.

This pattern rests nicely in the surface film even when water-proofed, as there is no hackle to make it sit up. The wings do not fold back and catch under the hook bend as do hackle-point wings, nor do they break off.

Occasionally a larger species of pale watery is seen hatching. The patterns I have described seem equally acceptable to trout at such times, but where large trout are expected, advantage may be taken to fish the same dressing on a larger hook, No 14.

Hook size is one of the difficulties for fishing the Test as it is today. Forty years ago, a four-pounder was as big as one could expect; now rainbows of more than twice that size are not uncommon and the record for the stretch I fish most is over 10 lb. It is difficult to control fish of this calibre on a No 16 or a No 14 hook, which cannot be fished delicately on a leader point thicker than about 3 lb breaking load. This combination makes success in a weedy river more a matter of luck than of skill, which is why at least some anglers tend more and more to fish large sedge flies on the surface and big nymphs, sometimes leaded, below it.

I find, however, that having caught my share of very large trout, I tend more and more to seek smaller specimens with the small flies associated traditionally with chalk-stream fishing, whenever a rise of duns or a fall of spinners gives one the opportunity.

I take care, though, to avoid making my preference an ethical matter. If the managers of Test and other chalk-stream fisheries are going to introduce monster trout, it is but reasonable for anglers to use flies and leaders that are adequate to catch them. It also seems to me sensible, when as is so often the case no hatch of fly occurs and trout are seen busily eating shrimps, to fish for them at the level at which they are feeding with an imitation of their chosen diet at that time.

Since most Test fisheries are now frequently and liberally stocked, there is no question of catching and injuring too many undersized trout nor of depriving fellow anglers of sport, if a rather catholic selection of wet and dry patterns is used. Because the little floater is perhaps the most enjoyable way, we need not go fishless when the opportunity to use it fails to present itself.

Different Types of Fly

Anglers new to trout-fishing cannot fail to be puzzled at the vast numbers of different artificial flies they read about and see in tackle shops, and also by the apparent inconsistency in books and articles about trout-fishing. One writer describes patterns that imitate or suggest natural insects as effectively as possible; another lists large lures that bear no resemblance to any living creature. A third will maintain that success depends entirely on presentation and the fly pattern is of no importance.

What follows is an attempt to explain these inconsistencies, based on what I have learned about trout in fifty years of catching a good many thousands of them. Call it theory or speculation if you like, but test it against your own experience, past, present and future.

A trout can be in any state of hunger from not wanting food at all to ravenous, and any degree in between.

What it is willing to eat, if willing it be, is determined by what food is available; but like most other fish, the greater the number of identical food items it finds and the smaller they are, the more the trout becomes preoccupied by them, though when more than one kind is available in large numbers, trout do show preferences.

Consequently, a trout that is willing to feed may be oblivious to all but one sort of food item, or it may be willing to take anything that

69

looks like food, or it may be feeding in a way that is between these extremes.

Obviously, when a trout is feeding selectively, eating only one kind of food, which is usually an insect of one kind or another, then the angler needs an artificial fly into which is built the features, or recognition points, by which the fish distinguishes that food item from others. In designing imitative artificial flies, it is for these recognition points that the fly-tyer should look. They are not easy to assess, but we have reason to believe that the most important involve a colour or colours. Size seems to be more important in floating than in sunk flies. There is evidence to show that shape is of little importance. In some cases a degree of exaggeration in one or more of the recognition points makes a fly more effective, and this can apply to behaviour or movement as well as to appearance.

There is also good reason to think that if enough recognition points are built into the artificial fly, trout will ignore points of difference, like a hundred legs instead of six and the usually very visible hook bend, point and barb. I do not wish to enlarge on this business of recognition points and deliberate exaggeration here; suffice it to say that trout feeding selectively often need an imitative fly pattern to catch them, and as there are many different insects on which the fish may feed in this way, the fly-fisher needs quite a range of patterns of this kind.

I should add, however, that selective trout may sometimes be caught with a large fly or lure which provokes them to attack it, through resentment of the invasion of their feeding area or the desire to eliminate competition. Anglers interested in the problems of fly design do not care to catch trout in that way, which they regard as rather like avoiding being beaten at chess by kicking the board off the table.

Trout that are not feeding selectively but are willing to feed can be taken on almost any fly pattern provided it is fished correctly and they can see it. This is by no means a minor point; in coloured or muddy water, the fly that can be seen at the greatest distance usually catches the most trout. Water colour varies, so a range of differently coloured flies or lures is needed to meet the different conditions that may be encountered.

As well as imitative flies and non-imitative, aggression-provoking lures, we have the so-called fancy flies. In many cases, these will be found to incorporate certain features that are in fact the recognition points of insects. Wet flies, and wet lake flies in particular, have been adulterated and standardised down the years to suit the convenience of the fly-tying trade, but in many instances they still retain these recognition points despite their having ceased to bear much superficial resemblance to the insects they were originally intended to imitate.

Some fancy flies are, however, difficult if not impossible to identify in respect of natural prototypes, and one can only assume that these are taken by hungry trout that are not feeding selectively, out of curiosity. Since trout live almost entirely on animal matter, and live creatures at that, anything that moves has at least one recognition feature, and that may induce a fish to take it, to see if it is in fact eatable. A trout that has never been hooked and lost or caught and returned has no reason to fear such an investigation, and most anglers will have seen fish take and then eject all sorts of inedible objects like matchsticks, cigarette ends, twigs and the like.

Since selective or preoccupied feeding by trout is induced by the presence of large numbers of small food items, it follows that it is on waters where these circumstances occur most often that a selection of imitative artificial flies are of most use to the angler. Conversely, where the trout food is scarce, or where it is in great variety but does not include any one organism in great numbers, the imitative patterns are not so necessary, though they will often catch trout.

So how many patterns and sizes of fly ought a beginner to acquire? I think the answer must be 'as many as he knows how and when to use'. One can spend half the day changing from one fly to another without success. The novice must ask himself why the fly he is using is not catching fish; is it because there are none where he has chosen to fish? Has he scared them? Is he fishing the fly correctly? There are many reasons for failure, other than fishing the wrong pattern of fly, and until they have all been eliminated, there is no point in changing, which only wastes time.

It is only when the trout are obviously feeding and refusing the fly in use that a change is clearly indicated, and then it ought to be possible to see, or to deduce from the behaviour of the fish, what it is that they are eating, whereupon a pattern to imitate or at least suggest the chosen item of diet is tried.

A range of books exists that can help the novice fly-fisher to identify the numerous insects and other items of trout food, and to select artificial flies designed to suggest these various creatures. The

71

literature also contains ranges of fancy flies and lures, and from these perhaps half a dozen can be chosen almost at random, since unselective trout will take any of them if they are fished correctly. To suit waters differently coloured, it is as well to include predominantly orange, white, yellow and black respectively, for four of the patterns.

In addition to what may be culled from the literature, local information is valuable and it comes free from the better tackle shops and from experienced fellow-anglers whom the novice meets at the waterside, from whom he should never fear to seek advice – when they have temporarily stopped fishing. The more experienced and successful an angler is, the more willing he will usually be found to help a beginner. A churlish refusal of help or advice, rare as it is, is an indication that the man has little advice worth giving.

The novice fly-fisher must understand that he has taken up a very complex sport in which there is no short cut to success, no magic fly that will catch trout anywhere and at any time. Knowledge of which patterns to tie, and how, when and where to use them, is built up over a long time and even the most experienced angler is all too conscious of the gaps in his knowledge. The novice has, however, the consolation that it is fun finding out. When he finds the right fly, fishes it right and puts some good fish on the bank, his pleasure will be greater by far than that enjoyed by the hard-bitten old veteran who has caught fish on that fly, in similar circumstances, dozens and dozens of times in the past.

Buzzers

By far the most common insects on all the reservoirs and man-made lakes that I have fished are the chironomids, alias midges, alias buzzers. There are many species and I think it likely that some of them remain to be identified and classified.

These insects comprise an important part of the diet of still-water trout, probably the most important part, since it is uncommon to catch a fish that has none in its stomach, and very common to find trout stomachs packed with them.

The life cycle is egg, larva, pupa, winged insect. The larva lives in the bottom mud eating detritus; the bloodworm is a well-known example, but in some species the larva is brown, in others olive, in others green. Attempts to imitate the larva have been made, with modest success. Among them is Arthur Cove's rubber-band fly.

I have devised a pattern that has caught a number of fish, but it is not one that professional tyers can usefully exploit. It is made by stretching a piece of alasticum wire between two fly-tying vices and then wrapping this with a strip of rubber, cut from a child's balloon, in overlapping turns that are stuck together with rubber solution. After this has set, the wire is withdrawn, leaving a thin, segmented, translucent rubber tube which can be cut into appropriate lengths and lashed on behind the eye of a suitable hook, with one turn of white ostrich herl ahead of it. This pattern is fished on a long leader so that it can be tweaked back just above the bottom. On occasions it works very well.

It is the next stage, however, the pupa, that is of greater importance to the stillwater trout-fisher. Examination of stomach contents of trout shows very clearly that it is at this stage that by far the greater proportion of the chironomids taken by trout are eaten, and consequently it is the pupa that the angler finds most profitable to imitate.

Very many different ways of imitating chironomid pupae have been tried and new ones are constantly being introduced. The issue is apt to be confused by the fact that, at times, trout will take almost anything, and in certain conditions one pupa imitation is as good as another.

A real chironomid pupa is translucent, so that a trout can see what colour it is regardless of the relative positions of the fish, the light source and the pupa.

If you tie an artificial pupa with an opaque body, it will catch trout in certain circumstances but not in others. Seen against the light, it will appear black and that will be acceptable to trout eating black pupae. Lit from behind the trout, or partly so, the colour of the opaque body will be visible to the trout and if it is the colour he wants, he will be likely to take it. If however he wants a colour other than black, he will not be likely to accept an opaque imitation that he sees against the light, even if it is of the right colour. Consequently it pays to design pupa imitations with translucent bodies, or bodies that provide an illusion of translucence, and there are several ways in which that may be accomplished.

One is to use bodies dubbed with dyed seal's fur, and such patterns are reasonably effective. There is considerable deviation from the appearance of the natural, which has a smooth body, not a hairy one, but it cannot be denied that hairy imitations often catch trout.

Another method consists in winding cellulite floss over a white-painted hook shank, as invented by J.W. Dunne for dry flies. When wet, a fine appearance of translucence is obtained, but such patterns are tedious for the professional tyer, and the floss stands up very poorly to the effects of trout teeth.

My own preference is for bodies of dyed feather fibre ribbed with stripped cock-hackle stalk. The fine, short whiskers of the feather fibre refract light, so that the colour can be seen whatever the relative positions of fish, fly and light, but the basic form and segmentation are retained. By winding the feather fibre over a whipped, varnished hook shank while the varnish is still wet, and ribbing on an opposite spiral, a very durable dressing is produced, and one that is commercially viable, an important consideration because the majority of fly-fishers have to depend upon professional fly-tyers for their supplies of artificials.

The patterns I use differ from one another only in respect of hook size and material colours, which is useful to the professional tyer and quite satisfactory to the trout!

You proceed as follows:

Take a bunch of long fibres from a white cock-hackle and bend these down on the back of the hook shank, leaving the thick ends projecting well ahead of the eye and the thin ends well past the bend. Take this binding, in touching turns, about one third of the way round the bend and there tie in the thin end of the white cock-hackle stalk, plus two or three strands of dyed feather fibre by their thin ends.

Wind the silk back along the shank to the point where the front half of the body will end and then varnish these turns of silk. Clear nail varnish is suitable but clear polyurethane is stronger.

Wind the feather fibre which you have twisted in touching turns to form the body – or abdomen – and secure with the silk. Wind the hackle stalk over it in open turns and secure.

Now tie in either two or three strands of peacock herl, or of appropriately coloured feather fibre, according to which species of pupa you are imitating, wind on the silk to just behind the eye; wind the herl over and over to form a fat thorax, tie down with the silk, and

74

finish with a whip-finish behind the eye, but ahead of the projecting white fibres.

Clip these white fibres short at both head and tail, apply a drop of varnish to the whip finish and your sooper-dooper-pooper is complete.

There are two exceptions to this basic system; one is a pupa found only occasionally, and not on all waters, whose imitation has a rib of narrow gold lurex instead of hackle stalk, and another needs a crimson-dyed hackle-stalk rib.

Here is a table of colours and hook sizes:

Colour of abdomen	Thorax	Rib	Hook sizes
Black	Peacock	White	10, 12, 14, 16
Claret	Peacock	White	10, 12
Red	Peacock	White	12
Green	Peacock	White	12, 16
Brown-olive	Brown feather fibre	White	12
Golden-olive	Peacock	Gold lurex	12, 14
Green-olive	Peacock	Crimson	8

I have no doubt that further study of the naturals will lead to other colour schemes for artificials; for example, some black pupae have red in their last two or three abdomen segments, though trout seem content with the Claret artificial when these are active.

I do not care for metal tinsels or threads to rib artificials; these increase sinking rates.

A great deal has been written about how to fish artificial chironomid pupae, the usual view being that they should be fished as near the surface as possible and moved only very slightly. This will undoubtedly succeed at times, but despite the limited ability of the natural to move, I catch more fish by moving the artificial quite quickly than by moving it slowly. I find the most successful technique, when fish can be seen breaking the surface, is to cast crosswind, ahead of individual fish, and then draw steadily, without tweaks or jerks.

I often fish a pupa as dropper and a Longhorn (which imitates a sedge pupa) on the point, since still-water trout frequently change from eating chironomids to eating sedges, and then back again to chironomids at dusk. The larger fly acts as a sea-anchor, causing the pupa to fish shallower when drawn at medium pace. This results in shallow fishing without having to grease the leader; I think a floating leader often scares fish, specially in bright light, even if moved only slowly. I should, however, add that artificial pupae do often succeed when moved almost imperceptibly on a leader greased all the way to the fly. John Goddard is a leading exponent of this technique and describes it in detail in *Trout Flies of Stillwaters*.

Occasionally the artificial pupa succeeds when allowed a sinking time of some 30 seconds, followed by a very slow, twitching retrieve.

I have never done much with artificial pupae fished on sinking fly-lines, though I believe others have.

In my experience, the chironomid in its winged form is not very attractive to trout, but I have taken fish occasionally with floating winged imitations, especially black ones. The best dressing I have devised so far is as follows:

> Body, black feather fibre, ribbed white cock-hackle stalk, wound double behind eye to form a fat thorax
> Wings, two grizzled badger cock-hackle points, set slanting well back, not reaching tail end of body
> Hackle, a natural black cock-hackle, rather long in fibre, not too many turns
> Tails, none
> Hook, 12 or 14

Other dry patterns that have occasionally caught me trout are exactly as above but with orange or green bodies and hackles. However, I doubt if the times when a floating imitation of the winged form will catch more fish than a pupa are anything but very rare.

Although the patterns and fishing methods I have described have been satisfactorily successful, I cannot pretend that finality in imitation or presentation has by any means been reached. On the contrary, I think a great deal remains to be learned about designing and fishing artificial chironomids. For example, there is a little olive-green pupa, needing a No 18 hook for size, that trout eat avidly, but I have never succeeded in devising an imitation that the fish will take.

In choosing which colour of pupa to fish, it helps to observe winged forms on the water or better still, to dip out natural pupa with a small muslin net, but in the absence of any such information I would first try the claret pupa, then black, then green. Where there is little or no weed, more than one pattern can be fished at a time, in which case the largest should be on the point.

Leader thickness should be chosen to suit the hook-size: about 0.009 in for size 12, 0.008 in for 14, 0.007 in for 16 hooks. When casting to visibly rising fish it is important that the leader goes under directly, so pull it through a ball of synthetic mud made by mixing fuller's earth with neat washing-up liquid.

Finally, never imagine that these small insects appeal only to small trout. I have found the stomachs of six-pounders absolutely packed with them.

Tying Your Own Flies

It astonishes me that so few trout and salmon anglers tie their own flies. The reasons they give for not doing so are numerous and varied, but except in the case of serious physical handicap, none of them are sound.

Any man who can knot a fly to his leader is perfectly capable of tying quite a wide selection of killing trout flies without any previous knowledge of, or practice in, the art of fly-tying.

It is true that there are many artificial flies that do need knowledge and skill to tie well. I would not expect a complete novice to make a good job, at his first attempt, of tying a pattern like Lunn's Particular, or a Winged Iron Blue. But then, I would not recommend such a person to devote his efforts to tying patterns such as these, or indeed any other pattern involving the more advanced skills of fly-tying.

It is, as I have said, easy to produce some very successful patterns with an absolute minimum of skill and knowledge, and if a man concentrates on these, he will be tying flies that he can use right from the start, and, without realising it, developing skills that will eventually make tying the more difficult patterns very much easier.

But first, the tools. To begin, all you need are the following:

1 vice; it need not be an expensive one
1 pair hackle pliers

1 dubbing needle
1 pair small pointed scissors

You can make the dubbing needle by forcing the eye end of a sewing needle into the end of a 2-in length of ¼-in dowel. A bit of twig of these approximate dimensions will do. As for the scissors, you may be able to borrow these from the lady of the house.

Start with the easiest pattern of all, the Chomper. For this you will need a hank of brown Raffene and some ostrich herl. Messrs Veniards, who will become lifelong friends if you pursue this pastime, will supply these materials; ask for ostrich herl dyed green and also amber, as well as plain white. Veniards will also sell you some tying silk, and I suggest that at first, brown will do all you need.

I leave the choice of sizes and types of hook to you, but one easy way is to go through your existing flies and strip the dressing from any that have become tatty and disreputable. This will usually provide enough eyed hooks to get you started.

Grip the hook in the vice so that its point is covered by the jaws, but the full length of the shank is exposed.

Take a piece of Raffene, wet, and stretch it. Lash it onto the shank of the hook with silk. No need to be neat and tidy about it. The lashing can be as crude as you like. Just leave at least 1½ in projecting past the hook bend; cut off the other end behind the eye.

Take two or three strands of the ostrich herl and bind them down near the start of the bend, where the Raffene emerges from its binding. Then wind the silk back along the shank in open turns, till it is a little behind the eye of the hook.

Now twist the strands of ostrich herl together and wind them in touching turns, round and round the shank, till you reach a point about ⅛ in behind the hook eye. Then grip the ends with your hackle pliers and let them hang, while you bend down the stuff with a few turns of your silk. Transfer the pliers to the silk and let them hang, keeping the silk taut, while you cut off the ends of the herl. Now re-damp the Raffene, pull it forwards to make a back for the fly, binding it down with the silk just behind the eye. Put two or three half hitches in the silk, apply a drop of quick-drying varnish and let it dry. Cut off the surplus silk, and your fly is finished. Some day you'll learn to make a whip finish, which is neater, but don't worry about that yet.

Tie some more Chompers in different colours and sizes. The three herl colours I've suggested, tied in sizes 14 up to 8, will give you a

range of flies from which one will catch you a trout or two on almost
any day and on any water. Right away you have made flies you can
use effectively, and there is nothing more encouraging to a novice fly-
tyer than to find his very first efforts are successful in catching trout.

When you have tied a few dozen Chompers in different colours and
sizes, you can tie a Partridge. Go and shoot a partridge, or get its
breast and flank feathers some other way. If you can't get them free,
Mr Veniard will oblige. Get some brown, some grey. Grey ones aren't
actually grey; they're speckled, black and white. You may now raid
the lady's sewing basket for bits of coloured silk, but I would also
recommend acquiring, again from the ubiquitous Mr Veniard, a little
fluorescent wool, in orange and in lime-green. The silk and the wool
are for body materials; you can tie partridge in a variety of lovely
colours, like green, red, orange, yellow and purple, and with either
the brown or the grey partridge hackle.

Tied in a range of sizes, these patterns will also catch you fish. I
suggest that if you fish for trout in still waters, you make a start with a
very easily tied one, which I call the Short Green Partridge. I suggest
this one because I've caught a lot of trout with it, including seven over
10 lb, and that alone ought to give you some confidence in it.

Grip a No 6 hook in your vice. Take a grey partridge-hackle feather
and pull off the fluff from around the end that was in the bird. Take a
bit of lime-green wool, which you will find consists of three twisted
strands. Unravel it so you have just one strand, with which you bind
the root of the hackle onto the hook shank, about ⅛ in behind the eye,
the root pointing towards the hook bend. After three or four touching
turns of wool, cut off any projecting feather root. Continue binding
till you reach a point on the shank opposite the point of the hook;
then wind the wool back, over the original turns, till you reach the
partridge feather again. Attach the hackle pliers to the wool and let
them hang to keep it taut, while you take a bit of your brown silk and
bind the wool down. You can then transfer the hackle pliers from
wool to silk and cut off the surplus wool.

Now take a half hitch in the silk, and transfer the pliers to the end
of the centre rib of the partridge feather. If it breaks, take a bigger bite
of it with the pliers. Holding the pliers, wind the feather twice round
the hook-shank, between the end of the wool body and the hook eye.
Only twice. Then use the silk to bind the feather end down, make
your half hitches, cut off the end of the feather and of the silk, apply
the usual drop of varnish, and you have a Short Green Partridge.

In all these operations, you may find it easier if you wax any silk you use; just pull it through a bit of solid fly-tyer's wax, quickly. Need I tell you who sells this wax? You can tie lots of these Partridge flies and they'll all catch fish; if one sort or size doesn't, try another. Don't worry if they, or your Chompers, look rather scruffy. The trout are far less critical than you.

At first, supplement your collection by buying ready-made examples of more difficult fly patterns, and concentrate on making your own easy ones. In time you will want to try your hand at the harder ones, but don't be too eager to do so. Stick at the Chompers and Partridges till you can tie a dozen of any size in an hour, every one exactly alike. Then you can start on more complex patterns, and you will find that they aren't really so difficult.

Land Insects

A good many years ago, an angler named Leonard West wrote a book about trout flies, in which he included a great number of terrestrial as well as water-bred insects. His book was largely ignored, probably because, at the time, dry-fly snobbery was prevalent. This was based not only on the premise that the fly must float, but also upon the notion that any angler should fish only for trout rising to identifiable natural insects, of which an imitation must be used.

A general rise by trout to land-bred insects is not very common, specially on rivers, and consequently little attention was paid to what West wrote. In addition, a great deal of what was written about fly-fishing at that time was all about chalk-streams, which in those days had frequent and plentiful hatches of aquatic insects.

Despite this, however, there has been a degree of recognition, for some 300 years, that trout often do eat land-bred insects, a fact that regular examination of their stomach contents will amply confirm. It is therefore rather odd that, of the vast array of artificial fly patterns that can now be found in the shops, a smaller percentage than ever before are intended to imitate terrestrial insects. It is of course equally true that only a small percentage of these flies are intended to imitate any kind of insect!

One favourite among the Victorian trout fly-fishers that seems to have disappeared from the regular professional dressers' lists is the Cowdung fly. It has not disappeared from the countryside, nor, at times, from the inside of trout stomachs. If you find yourself fishing from a field where there are cows or bullocks, and especially when a breeze is blowing, you may catch trout very successfully with an imitation Cowdung fly.

Tie it on a No 12 or No 14 hook, with a body of khaki wool spun on to olive silk, rather fat; a brown-olive hackle and a wing made of a bunch of dun hackle fibres, clipped flush with the hook bend. And I mean dun; not the battleship blue-grey dyed hackle that has come to be known as blue dun. The true dun colour is a kind of pale sepia.

Trout often take this pattern avidly, be it sunk or floating. They are equally keen on the Hawthorn fly, which is in considerable evidence on some waters at the same time as the mayfly, or thereabouts. Indeed, so keen are the trout on it at times that they will take a very simple artificial, having no more than a black floss body and a black hackle. I fancy that when they have eaten great numbers of these insects, they become fussier, and then a fatter body, more nearly resembling that of the real insect, may be more acceptable, specially if it includes a dun wing and a couple of knotted black feather fibres to imitate the long rear legs.

It has a near relation, has the Hawthorn fly, usually found around acid lochs where the heather grows, which is why it is called the heather fly, when it isn't called the bloody doctor. It's just like the hawthorn fly except that the upper joints of its legs are rich red. So you tie in some legs made of crimson-dyed pheasant-tail fibres and there you have it.

Another useful land insect, on both lake and river, at times only, is the hover, or drone, fly. It looks like a slim wasp, hovers like a helicopter and when freshly hatched has bright red eyes. Seasons may pass on some waters without this insect appearing in sufficient numbers to interest the trout; then comes a summer when drone flies are seen everywhere and the artificial becomes positively deadly. For that reason I always carry half a dozen in my box. It has a fat body with alternate black and yellow rings, of clipped dyed ostrich herl, a pale ginger hackle, dun wing and a turn of crimson ostrich herl at the head, in front of the wings and hackle. Like the flies already described, it is effective whether fished wet or dry.

Sometimes beetles of various kinds appear in huge numbers and the trout become preoccupied with eating them. In my childhood, huge beetles, cockchafers, were very common, but I haven't seen one of those for years. What I do often see are small beetles, the familiar ladybirds or small black beetles of similar shape. These are very easily imitated; you make a fat body of feather fibre, peacock herl or clipped ostrich herl, and then tie in a bunch of suitable feather fibre over the back of it, tied in at the head and again at the bend, to imitate the wing cases; chestnut colour for the ladybird, black for the small black beetle. Trout don't mind omission of the ladybird's spots!

One of the few land insects that has featured frequently in fly-fishing literature is the ant. In fact, it is quite rare for any angler to have the chance to cash in on a flight of ants; I cannot remember more than four or five occasions in my own lifetime. There's no doubt, however, that trout eat flying ants with great relish when they have the chance to do so, and it is therefore wise to have a few imitations, just in case the opportunity to use them should occur.

It is necessary to imitate both red and black ants, and the most common mistake is to tie them too small. I fancy that fly-dressers have mental pictures of worker ants and dress artificials about that size, when in fact the flying ant is very much bigger, and needs a No 12 or even No 10 hook to dress natural size.

Another land insect that has not been totally neglected is the daddy-long-legs, or crane-fly. There are several species, some much larger than others, but in practical fishing a pattern tied on a No 8 long-shank hook is all that is needed. For decades, I tied these things with legs spread all round, and caught only occasional fish with them. It was only when I realised that either in flight or in the water, the legs of these insects all trail backwards, that I evolved a pattern that proved thoroughly successful. I now find that for some unknown and apparently illogical reason, a dressing with a green fluorescent body is even more effective. Truly, we have much to learn about trout vision and the responses provoked by it.

Among the most effective flies for catching trout of above average size are imitations of moths, especially when used at dusk. There is a huge variety of moths, and fortunately trout seem seldom, if ever, to feed selectively on them. I only use two artificials and it can be argued that neither looks very much like a moth; one is the Ghost Swift, or Chicken, predominantly white, and the other, which may be taken either for a brown moth or a great red sedge, is made of pheasant-tail fibres and natural red cock-hackle; both are on No 8 long-shank hooks.

There are many more land insects that can be imitated with advantage: a great range of beetles, several sorts of grasshopper, bluebottles, houseflies, earwigs, bumble bees, and a whole range of caterpillars. As well as insects, there are spiders of many sorts. All these creatures are often found inside trout, and their imitations can catch trout. Terrestrial insects are worthy of more study, with a view to imitation, than is often accorded to them.

Damsel Fly – Dry

On the smaller lakes, blue damsel flies are often very numerous, and are readily eaten by trout both in their nymphal and winged forms. We already have a variety of imitations of the nymph, but relatively few of the winged insect.

The temptation to the fly-dresser is to attempt a very exact imitation of these beautiful creatures, but it is only necessary to incorporate the basic points of recognition for the fly to be entirely effective.

The body of my pattern is made of bright Cambridge-blue floss, soaked in Durofix diluted with amyl acetate. This preserves the colour and prevents it from either darkening or becoming translucent when wet. The body is ribbed with black sewing silk.

The simple wing consists of fibres from a cree or cuckoo cockhackle, tied on in a bunch. By manipulating the bunch, one can move some of the fibres lengthways relative to others, to reduce the barred effect and produce more of a speckled appearance. The hackle should be very sparse and made from any black feather that has rather thick fibres, such as a black hen-breast feather. Two turns is enough. The tying silk is black.

I have seen some much more elegant-looking imitations of the damsel fly than this, but for some reason the wings are usually tied horizontal and at right angles to the body, a position they only assume in the real insect when it is in flight. When at rest or under water, they lie along the abdomen.

For some curious reason, some anglers have begun calling this insect the damosel. Dante Gabriel Rossetti's 'Blessed Damozel' was quite a different kind of animal, difficult to imitate with fly-tying materials. (Even the AA couldn't supply *seven* stars!)

Some damsel flies have brown or green bodies; the former is simply imitated with a pheasant-tail body, the latter with a body of light green floss.

Leaded Nymphs

Since an article of mine about leaded flies appeared in *Shooting Times*, quite a few anglers have written or 'phoned for more information about them, especially in respect of patterns.

It must be explained right away that there is no way of incorporating sufficient lead in a very small fly. This means that imitations of small nymphs of the olives, the blue-winged olive, the iron blue and the pale watery, are eliminated if you want to fish deep in any but the slowest current or the shallow runs.

Nymphs of this type are tied on size 14, 15 and 16 hooks as a rule, and such hooks will accommodate only one layer of lead foil along the length of the hook shank, plus two more small pieces under the thorax. This will give a faster sinking rate than the more usual copper wire, but it is nothing like fast enough to reach the bottom of a quick run, 4 or 5 ft deep, in a river like the Test.

So, if you want to reach trout in that sort of situation, you have to use a much bigger fly. The most useful patterns for water of this sort are the mayfly nymph, the damsel larva (or nymph) and the shrimp.

Oddly enough, the artificial mayfly nymph will catch trout at any time of the season. This does not mean that trout will accept it every day, or that every trout will take it on any day. But you are just as likely to catch fish with it in September as in April. The best time for it is May, and probably it would be deadliest of all when the natural mayflies are hatching, but at that time it becomes unnecessary, because you can uses a dry fly. I must stress here that, while I have no doubt that an angler could do well using none but leaded flies, I use them only when there is no prospect of rising fish; not for ethical reasons but because in a rise, I find the dry fly not only more enjoyable to use, but also a good deal easier. With a dry fly, the problem of placement is two-dimensional; with a weighted nymph or shrimp it is three-dimensional and correspondingly more difficult.

The artificial mayfly nymph uses only three materials: pale yellow-ish-buff wool, pheasant-tail fibres and brown tying silk. Build up the lead underbody on a No 8 long-shank hook. Tie in half a dozen pheasant-tail fibres for the tails, rather short. Tie in the wool and an extra strand of silk for ribbing – or you can use a strand of brown-dyed 4-lb b.s. monofil, which is stronger.

Wind the wool tightly to about two-thirds of the way between the start of the hook bend and the eye and rib it with the ribbing material, using fairly close turns to produce about five or six 'segments'. The first turns of ribbing should be in two closely spaced sets, so as to produce the appearance of two brown bands at the rear end of the abdomen, the rest of the ribbing turns being single. Rib on the opposite spiral to the wool.

Next, tie in a generous bunch of pheasant-tail fibres with their points forward, extending far enough beyond the hook eye to allow them to be stroked back and secured to imitate legs. Then wind on more turns of wool, which will not be ribbed, to form the thorax, stopping short of the hook eye, to allow room to finish. Set the 'legs' in position with a figure-of-eight binding, then bring the butts of the pheasant-tail fibres forwards, to imitate the wing-cases of the natural, and tie down firmly just behind the eye. Put a drop of varnish in here before building up a head with the tying silk and whip-finishing.

The next step is to prick out the wool between each of the single turns of ribbing on the abdomen, in generous bunches, on each side of the body; not on the back or underside, only along each side. Having pricked them out, trim with scissors to equal length.

Finally, run a streak of clear varnish along the back of the abdomen and all along the underside from tail to hook-eye, and your mayfly nymph is finished. It has required rather a long explanation, but it is really quite an easy job, though it takes time. When the varnish is nearly dry, you can flatten any 'whiskers' on back and underside with your fingers.

By comparison the Damsel nymph is much easier. Actually, it ends up much fatter than a real damsel nymph, and more resembles the larvae of water beetles and dragonflies! Tie in a few green-dyed feather fibres as tails; then dub your brown tying silk with a mixture of yellow, orange, blue and green wool, thoroughly mixed. Also tie in a piece of brown silk or monofil at the tail.

Run the dubbed silk all the way to just behind the hook-eye; rib; tie in a brown partridge hackle and wind it at the head, rather sparse. Secure, cut off waste and whip-finish, and there is your Damsel nymph; the same hook as for the mayfly.

A useful blank-saver is a similarly tied pattern using only orange wool. That will sometimes tempt a fish that has refused other patterns.

The Leaded Shrimp can be tied on normal-shank hooks, sizes 12 to 8 inclusive. The deeper and faster the water, the larger is the size you fish.

Build up the underbody with layers of lead strip in the usual way, taking the first layer about one third of the way round the hook bend. Dub the silk with fawn or olive wool and tie in a big ginger cock-hackle at the rear end. Wind the dubbing to just behind the eye and rib with open spirals of the cock-hackle. Tie down, cut off waste, finish the head.

Now clip off all the projecting cock-hackle fibres on the back and sides, leaving only those that point downwards, which you clip to a length a little more than the gape of the hook.

Finally, treat the back to successive coats of clear varnish, till it is smooth and glossy.

An alternative is to secure a strip of polythene over the back, but it is much more fragile than hard-dried varnish.

You can tie a few shrimps with either orange or yellow wool and a hackle of corresponding colour, which may get you a fish when other patterns have failed. A friend of mine ties a black version which he tells me is often successful.

While the Leaded Shrimp is good for trout, there are times when it is positively deadly for grayling. Beware fishing it down and across at the tail of a pool in a trout river – trout will hit it with tremendous violence and, if you are not very alert, break the leader point as if it were horsehair. It doesn't take an outsized trout to do it.

Don't be tempted, in making these flies, to save time by winding lead wire or strip round and round the hook shank. Not only does this effectively narrow the gape and impede secure hooking; it also throws away the advantage which piling successive strips on the back of the shank gives you, of causing the fly to fish hook point up, which minimises catching weeds or snags on the bottom.

For the benefit of readers who missed my original article, lead is built up by winding strips of wine-bottle foil on the back of the shank,

FLIES

each strip being a little shorter and a little wider than its predecessor. The last strip is as long as the first, but pointed at each end. The combined effect is a nicely tapered lead underbody, over which the rest of the dressing is applied.

Dry Flies

It is quite amazing how beliefs held by anglers are repeated time and again, in articles, books and in discussion, until they become accepted as basic truths, so that anyone who questions them is considered heretical.

Of nothing is this more true than of the structure and effect of the dry fly. The most common kind is based on a combination of fallacies.

The first of these is that the natural insect rests on the surface film with only its feet touching. Everyone says so and for a long time I used to believe it. Eventually my belief was shaken by what I saw when swimming under water, and I constructed a plastic washing-up basin with a sheet of glass let into its bottom. This showed that newly-hatched upwinged flies (Ephemeridae) rest on the surface with part of the underside of their bodies touching it, as well as the feet.

We have been told constantly that the hackles of artificial dry flies must be stiff and sparkling, so as to lift the bodies clear of the surface – like the real insect – and to produce a pattern in the surface film that imitates that produced by the real insect's feet. As I've said, the body of the real insect is not in fact clear of the surface; and the pattern produced by a hackle in no way resembles that produced by the feet of an insect. Put the two, real and artificial, on the surface, and examine them from below, it will be seen that the difference is quite startling.

Why, in any case, should the hackle be sparkling? Not a single part of a newly hatched dun sparkles. Its 'finish' is uniformly matt, though the body has a degree of translucence.

So obsessed have fly-fishers become with the belief that dry-fly hackles should be stiff and sparkling that such hackles are now described as 'good', and ridiculous prices are paid for them. Some fly-dressers seem to prize their collections of cock capes so highly that it is a wonder how they can bring themselves to remove a single feather with which to tie a fly.

The truth is that no one needs a stiff, sparkling hackle from an ancient cock to make a good dry fly. As Swisher and Richards have shown in their book *Selective Trout*, you don't really need hackles at all. Modern waterproofing liquids, containing wax and silicones dissolved in a suitable volatile liquid, are so effective that cottonwool or blotting-paper, proofed with them, will sit on the water's surface indefinitely. When we were testing a proofing liquid before deciding whether it was good enough to market, I had a small ball of cottonwool sitting on the surface of a water-filled jam jar for more than a year.

A dry fly with a body made of dubbed wool, fur or hair, pricked out at the thorax, will float entirely satisfactorily, and produce a pattern in the surface film much more like that of a real insect than will a fly with a conventional hackle. Not that it matters, because trout are far less discriminating than anglers, and are satisfied if they can detect a few simple points of resemblance to the natural insect in which they are feeding. If they do, they will ignore quite blatant points of difference. The conventional dry fly catches trout and has been doing so for more than a century – but it does not need sparkling stiff hackles to do it.

So obsessed are fly-fishers with this kind of hackle that they apply it almost universally to imitations of the spent spinner stage of ephemerid flies. I confess that in the past I was sufficiently brain-washed to do so myself. This despite the fact that spent spinners lie with their wings flat on the surface, and the entire length of their bodies on the surface too. So why try to raise them above it?

Not that ultra-stiff hackles really do lift dry flies high above the surface. The truth is that the stiff hackle-fibre penetrates the surface film more readily than the soft, flexible fibre whose tip bends and thus spreads the load it carries over a wider area. Paradoxically, the failure of the stiff hackle fibre to lift the body and wings of the artificial spent spinner clear of the surface may be the reason why patterns tied with it are still quite effective for catching trout. If they floated as their designers intended, they might not be.

Many anglers continue to tie small spent spinners with wings made from whole hackle points, which have a habit of becoming caught under the bend of the hook. It is really better to construct the wings from a bunch of either hackle fibres or fur fibres, divided by a figure-of-eight binding and slanted forwards, in two horizontal bunches, at about 45 degrees to the shank of the hook. The stresses of casting bring them back to a position more or less at right angles to the body of the fly, but the initial angle resists their going back much farther and avoids the trouble to which whole hackle points are prone.

Who needs cock-hackles of any sort? The skin of a full-furred white rabbit cut into pieces, each of which is dyed a suitable colour, will provide long guard-hairs for wings and tails, while the softer under-fur makes a fine dubbing for bodies. Pinches of different colours can be mixed like paints to produce an almost unlimited colour range, while shades can be regulated by adding white. Still more effects can be obtained by adding a little wild rabbit, mole, hare or water-vole fur.

Using fur dubbing makes it perfectly easy to tie flies in which the thorax is darker than the abdomen, which is the case with most upwinged flies; and if no cock-hackle is wound on, the colour and also the shape of the entire fly body can be more accurately imitated, which is at least encouraging for those anglers who imagine that such niceties will help them to catch trout.

We come down, therefore, to this: that the only kind of fly for which glassy, sparkling, stiff cock-hackles are needed is the sort that enthusiastic fly-dressers enter in fly-tying contests, judged by men who still hold to the popular fallacies about what constitutes a good dry fly. If these contests were judged by trout, the results might be very different!

Tandem Lures

Joining hooks in making tandem lures seems still to present problems to many fly-dressers. I can honestly say that I have found a method that is entirely satisfactory, and is neither difficult nor time-consuming.

The joining material consists of a three-strand plait of ordinary nylon monofil. I use 12-lb b.s. for No 8 hooks and 15-lb b.s. for No 6s. It doesn't take long to plait a couple of feet of this, after which you hang it up by one end, with a weight at the other, and varnish it. You can use polyurethane or Vycoat. This not only makes the plait stiffer but also assists in adhesion to hook shanks. If you're worried, you can leave the plait unvarnished and use Araldite as an adhesive, but my tandems are all right with polyurethane. Don't use cyanoacrylic adhesive, as it won't stand up to soaking.

I start with the rear hook, either an up-eyed one, or one from which the down-eye has been broken. Starting at the end of the shank, I run an open spiral along the shank towards the bend to a point just short of opposite the hook point. There, the tying in of the plait begins and continues for a few close turns away from the shank end. Four or five firm turns of the Dacron thread are made, then any projecting ends of nylon plait are trimmed close. Next, tails, if any, body material and ribbing material are tied in.

Varnish is applied to the open turns of Dacron, and the Dacron is then used to bend down the plait, in tight touching turns up to near the end of the shank. The body and rib are now wound on, secured and a whip finish made. I usually add another coat of varnish over the turns of Dacron before winding body and rib, and the work proceeds while the varnish is wet.

The front hook is attached and its body formed in exactly the same way, leaving room behind the eye for tying in wing and throat hackle. The shorter the piece of plait between the two hooks, the stiffer it will be, and there's no advantage in making it longer than about ⅜ in.

I've tried dozens of methods of joining tandem hooks and none has been as good as the plait. Here are some of the alternatives that failed. Wire, whether single-strand, multi-strand, cable-laid or nylon-coated, fails very quickly due to fatigue fracture, probably caused by the stresses in turnover when it is cast.

Single-strand nylon is not stiff enough unless you use a very thick sample, and then it becomes difficult to whip it securely to hook-shanks. Expedients like serrating the nylon with pliers, doubling back and whipping down ends are all unreliable and time-consuming, and it is difficult to ensure that the hooks are in line.

Most of my lures are tied with two long-, but not ultra-long, shank hooks, the front one with a straight eye, the rear one with none.

There seems to me to be no advantage in using three hooks, unless you are making a very large tandem lure, more than 3 in long. Nor do I see any advantage in having hooks pointing up and down.

Some sea-trout anglers like tandem lures with one good-sized hook at the front and a small treble at the rear. It's always seemed to me that they might just as well use tube-flies; but if you want to make one

90

of these single-treble affairs, use a taper-shank treble and whip a single strand of 12-lb nylon to its shank. Then pass another strand around where the bends spread out. Lay its ends along the shank and whip down. Varnish the whipping. It isn't usual to put tails, body or ribbing on this rear treble but you can if you like. Then plait the three strands, and whip to the front hook in the usual way. The fact that one strand isn't very firmly secured doesn't matter; two 12-lb strands are strong enough, and the third is only there because you can't plait two.

I've given up using tandem lures for trout now, but I'd learned how to construct them properly before I decided on that. Now you know how to do it – if you want them.

Points of Difference

We read a good deal nowadays about fly-fishing for trout, but very little of it seems to me to show a real grasp of what makes a trout take an artificial fly. There's a lot of loose terminology tossed about, like 'imitation', 'sparkle', 'selective feeding' and so forth, and I admit freely that I am as guilty as others in this respect.

What do we mean by selective feeding? Well, if trout, or indeed other species of fish, see a large number of food items that are all alike, they tend to feed on them, and to ignore other kinds of food that are available at the same time but in lesser numbers. I use the word 'tend' because there are exceptions that seem to be due to preference. For example, trout seem to be especially fond of iron blues and will often eat them, even when they are outnumbered by insects of some other species. Another example is the turkey brown, which trout seem to reject even when it is present in large numbers.

Despite these exceptions, however, the generality holds good that trout tend to feed selectively when large numbers of insects of the same species, or other food organisms, are present.

This means that the fish are able to distinguish very easily between different species of insects, even when they are very similar. It is clear that they need not rely upon either shape or size to do so, because there is little if any difference in shape or size between iron blues and some kinds of pale watery. There is ample evidence to show that colour is a very important recognition feature. Indeed, it is probably the most important.

We hear talk about what is called 'exact imitation'; but obviously, really exact imitation is impossible. So why does a trout ever take an artificial fly when feeding selectively, since the differences between the natural and the artificial are so plain to see? Remember, the trout is easily able to discriminate between insects of different species which, however, resemble one another in our eyes much more than our artificials resemble natural insects.

Perhaps we can arrive at an answer by means of an analogy. Europeans often say that Chinese people all look alike. This is because Europeans first notice the facial characteristics that the Chinese have in common, the points of resemblance. The Chinese themselves, however, relegate these points of resemblance and, in order to distinguish between one another, look for the points of difference, of which there are plenty.

When a trout is feeding selectively on a particular species of insect, its brain is 'programmed' to notice the points of resemblance in that species of insect. Provided that an artificial fly incorporates enough of these points of resemblance, the trout relegates the points of difference, ignores them, and accepts the artificial. If this were not so, it would be impossible to catch a selectively feeding trout on an artificial fly.

The act of the fly-tyer therefore involves assessing what are the points of resemblance by which the trout recognises a kind of insect, and finding means of incorporating them in the artificial, using the materials at his disposal.

It is interesting to notice that he can never avoid also incorporating points of difference; and if a trout is captured and released, that trout will in future notice these points of difference and reject that particular pattern of artificial as a rule. Exceptions may be encountered that should not be taken to invalidate this general principle.

That the above is an over-simplification is admitted, and there is another factor that has to be considered. Both insects and trout do exist. They exist because, over many millions of years, they have acquired characteristics by evolutionary processes that have enabled their species to survive. The insects, of the sorts in which we and the trout are interested, have not evolved so as to be as attractive as possible to the trout. Indeed we may think that the appearance of many if not all of them involves some element of camouflage.

The trout, for its part, has evolved senses and perceptions that have enabled it too to survive, and it does eat insects, but not all, or they would be exterminated. It therefore seems possible that some exaggeration of the points by which trout recognise insects may make an artificial even *more* attractive to the trout than the natural insects themselves.

It is possible to exaggerate appearance in a number of ways. One can copy the colour or colours of the natural but make them brighter; one can add an extra element of colour; or one can exaggerate movement. Possibly because size and shape are less important as recognition factors to the trout, especially in the case of sunk flies, exaggeration in these areas has not proved successful, though it is worth remembering, in the interests of more secure hooking, that an artificial that is appreciably larger than the natural often proves acceptable, provided other recognition points are present.

This must not be taken to mean that size and shape are of no importance whatever; and it is important to realise the difference between overall shape and what might be called elements of shape. For example a Fore-and-aft Mayfly differs greatly from a real mayfly in overall shape, but the elements are present. The body is there, and the hackles, which suggest wings, are there too.

In some instances, colour and shape become in a sense interwoven. The female caperer carries an egg sac, yellowish in colour, at the rear end of the abdomen. For some unexplained reason, William Lunn's pattern to imitate this insect has a yellow band halfway along its abdomen. The trout find this perfectly acceptable, but is it a deviation in terms of shape, or of colour?

What is beyond doubt is that the presence of the yellowish touch makes the fly more acceptable to trout, wherever you put it; and there is a good deal of evidence to show that by exaggeration of the yellow, and the use of d.r.f. material for it, the acceptability is further increased.

When we come to fish that are not feeding selectively, but are willing to feed, it is much more difficult to arrive at conclusions about trends in fly or lure designs. There is, though, the point that if, as some suppose, a trout mistakes a Bucktail or Streamer for a small fish, then we should remember that a real small fish is camouflaged, and our lures may be more attractive if we omit such elements in their dressing as imitate the camouflage aspects of the real fish. The effectiveness of basically monochromatic patterns such as the Whisky Fly, Sweeney Todd and Mrs Palmer lend weight to the above theory.

Fly-fishing is an ancient art, but it still offers enormous scope for development, especially if we realise that the apparent logic of attempting to imitate exactly the insect or other animal that the trout eats is false; and also, that debate about the relative importance of imitation and presentation is sterile, since presentation is just one aspect of imitation.

Sedges

Sedge flies are very numerous on every kind of unpolluted water and are therefore important to the reservoir trout-fisher. There are many species, but from the point of view of the angler or the fly-tyer, similarities between species are such that only a few artificials are needed.

The life-cycle of sedge flies is as follows. On emerging from the egg, the larva builds itself a case. Different species choose different materials for this, and a few uncommon species are free-swimming in the larval stage. The larvae in their cases are called caddises.

After reaching full size, these larvae seal their cases while they transform into pupae, in which state they emerge from their cases, swim to the surface and transform into a winged insect, which usually flies to the bank and sits about on bank-side vegetation until it is time to mate. After mating, which in most species takes place on the wing over the water, the females drop their eggs onto the surface, completing the cycle.

Trout eat these insects at all stages, but the extent to which they do so depends on the insect concerned. The smaller sedges, which include the common brown silverhorns, black silverhorns and the grousewing, are not, in my experience, eaten extensively in the winged state. Larger sedges are.

All kinds are eaten in large quantities in the larval and pupal stages. In the first few months of the season, that is until the end of May, trout eat the cased larvae, specially the sort that make cases of sand or other hard kinds of debris. Since caddises are not very mobile, they are usually found over bottoms consisting of suitable material for case-making, mainly sand or gravel. Trout eating these caddises seem willing to take artificial flies imitating the pupal stage, and a suitable dressing, called the Longhorn, on a No 10 hook, is:

> Body, rear two thirds sea-green or amber ostrich herl ribbed with gold thread, front one third sepia or chestnut ostrich herl
> Hackle, brown partridge

Horns, two pheasant-tail fibres, twice as long as the hook, tied in slanting backwards.

There are four possible combinations of amber, green, sepia and chestnut, and there is a natural sedge pupa to which each combination corresponds. I have killed far more trout on the green and sepia than on any of the others; amber and sepia is the next highest scorer. These dressings can be leaded for fishing deep, or unleaded for use later in the season when the pupae are coming up to transform to the winged stage.

From June onwards, there are opportunities to catch trout on imitations of the winged sedge, fished dry. This applies particularly to the large sedges. The artificials can be dressed on a No 8 or more commonly No 10 round-bend long-shank hook, with feather-fibre bodies of green or chestnut, ginger cock-hackle fibre wings clipped square, flush with the bend of the hook, and plenty of ginger or natural red cock-hackles at the head. Occasionally, a wing of partridge-tail-feather fibres does well. With modern floatant liquids, body hackles are neither necessary nor desirable. A tip of orange d.f. wool at the tail end of the body may add to the attraction.

By far the best chance of catching trout on the larger sedges is when they are hatching. The pupae come up from where they live, in calm conditions. Therefore, go and fish where the water over a sandy bottom is calm. Start with a Longhorn, and change to the dry imitation when you see naturals taken on the surface. Do not move the dry artificial slowly. Either move it very fast, skimming over the surface, or else just let it sit without any movement at all.

The usual time for these sedges to hatch is at evening, but on a calm day following a good hatch the previous evening, you can often catch trout by the simple expedient of casting out an artificial sedge and letting it lie on the surface. It can work at any time of the day – the take is usually both unexpected and explosive, and it is all too easy to be broken when it occurs. It is also easy to strike too soon or too violently.

It does not, in my experience, pay to fish floating imitations of the smaller sedges. Artificial pupae do well, and often enough, copies of the winged form fished sunk. Here are some dressings which, on a No 12 or 14 hook, succeed often when trout are moving near the surface and you can see silverhorns or grousewings hovering over the water.

First the pupae, tied shaped rather like an ephemerid nymph, without tails or with two very short tail fibres. The abdomen is brown feather fibre ribbed with white cock-hackle stalk; the wing cases are brown feather fibre, and the thorax is amber or green d.f. wool tied fat. A brown-olive cock-hackle is wound just behind the hook eye and divided into two short, horizontal, backward-sloping bunches. Whether the orange or the green succeed best depends on which small sedge is on the water: green for black and brown silverhorns, orange for the grousewing.

The winged form, fished wet, is similar except that instead of wing-cases, you use a bunched wing of feather fibre of appropriate colour and two long pheasant-tail fibres to imitate the antennae of the insect.

Sometimes there is a mad rise to small sedges at the edge of the ripple off the weather shore, presumably to insects that have left bank-side vegetation to mate and lay their eggs. You catch few fish during this sort of rise, but as the trout are not very interested in anything else, you may as well persevere with either an imitation of the pupa or of the winged fly, or, if you like, one of each on your leader. You may get a fish or two, but nowhere near as many as the behaviour of the trout will lead you to expect.

Beware, at dusk, of the change by trout from eating sedges to eating midge pupae or caenis. This can often happen without any apparent change in the number or behaviour of rising fish, and if you fail to spot it, you can fish on with a dry sedge or a sedge pupa, among rising fish, wondering why they won't take. One way of avoiding this is to put a midge pupa on the point and a dry sedge on as a dropper, but that doesn't help if it is caenis the trout are eating.

Well, you can't win 'em all; and it remains a fact that the stillwater trout-fisher who understands sedges and how to fish imitations of them in their various stages will have lots of fun and catch many trout that he otherwise wouldn't.

Floating Flies

You very rarely see an angler using a floating fly on trout lakes and reservoirs, but sometimes certain patterns that float can catch far more fish than sunk flies.

Of all the dry patterns, the one that scores most often is the Red Sedge. There are many patterns, but I think my own is the best yet; if I didn't think so, I wouldn't tie it this way:

End of body, a turn of arc chrome fluorescent wool
Body, chestnut-coloured pheasant-tail fibre, three or four
    strands wound over wet varnish.
Wing, a bunch of natural red cock-hackle fibres, tied slanting
    well back over the body and clipped off flush with the hook
    bend
Head hackle, natural red cock
Hook, No 10 or 12

I've caught hundreds and hundreds of trout with this. You can let it
sit or you can skim it over the surface; try both ways and see which
does best on the day. After catching a few fish, it may sink. Before
reproofing it, try a few casts fishing it wet, retrieving it at a medium
pace.

Sometimes you'll see a few real sedges of unusual size, from 1 to
1¼ in. long. This is the great red sedge, and whenever you see it, tie
on a outsize version of the fly I've just described, tied on a No 8 long-
shank hook. You may connect with an outsize trout. I have, many
times.

Sedges are specially good in the evening and for the first hour of
darkness, both on rivers and lakes. You can tell when trout like eating
the real flies, because they rise with an emphatic chomp! and a bit of a
splash, unlike the quiet rises to midge pupae, caenis or the spinners of
lake and pond olives.

At this time of day, there's another very killing floater that I
invented thirty years ago:

Body, six or seven strands white ostrich herl ribbed with a cream
    cock-hackle
Wing, a bunch of swan secondary wing fibres
Head hackle, a natural ginger cock wound ahead of a cream
    cock
Hook, No 8 long-shank.

Let it sit or skim it; try both methods to see which the trout prefer. As
with the sedges, some evenings one scores better, sometimes the
other.

Then there's the Rasputin. Cut out a little block of fine-grain
polyethylene foam, slit it and glue it onto the whipped shank of a
No 6 long-shank hook. When the glue has set, carve or clip it to a fat

carrot shape, leaving ample room between body and eye. There, wind a ginger cock-hackle and divide it into two horizontal bunches with a figure-of-eight binding. Finally, give it a back of speckled-feather fibre, preferably mottled turkey, extending back to make a tail and tied down behind the body, and again between hackle bunches and hook eye.

This thing floats indefinitely and needs no waterproofing. Let it sit, or pull it across the surface. When trout are taking coarse fish fry, the Rasputin can be absolutely deadly, but I've caught trout with it from lakes where no coarse fish exist. They'll smash at it and if not hooked, will come again and again, till the hook takes a hold. It'll catch chub, too. It's much easier to make than you might think; if you take time and care to shape the body perfectly, it'll look nicer but it won't catch trout any better than if its body is only cut roughly to shape.

Perhaps not everyone would agree to this thing being called a fly, but I've never been told I can't use it on any lake or reservoir, and if I were a fishery manager, I'd rather see anglers using Rasputins than any two- or three-hook lures.

Another very deadly dry fly is the artificial daddy-long-legs. Don't tie or buy the sort with plastic detached bodies; they're bad hookers. I have to admit that my pattern is tedious and time-consuming to tie because it has eight legs, each a pheasant-tail fibre with two knots in it. The real insect has only six legs but the artificial legs sometimes get broken off or cut by trout teeth, so I start with eight. Trout can't count!

> Body, any brownish or earthy-coloured feather fibre
> Wings, a pair of badger cuckoo or dun cock-hackle points
> Hackle, ginger or ginger cree
> Legs, as described, all trailing backwards (that is important, I think. When you see the real insect sitting on the bank or scrambling about your window the legs stick out all round but when that fly is on the water, they all trail)
> Double up the body material round the wing and leg roots to imitate the thorax.

Never pull this one. Just let it sit or, in rough water, bounce it on the wave tops; but I repeat, never pull it to make a wake on the surface. Trout will follow it if you do that, but seldom take. So just let it sit, and mend line or recast if wind or drift makes it drag.

Where it's allowed you can use a long rod and a blowline, and dap. If you tie the Daddy as I've recommended, I'll back it to catch as many trout as a dapped natural. In fact, because it saves time that you'd otherwise spend catching naturals and getting them on the hook without losing half their legs, it will probably catch you a lot more.

Try it whenever you see natural daddies about, even if there are only few of them. Once trout have eaten a few real ones, they're eager for more. But if you buy these Daddies to my pattern ready-made, don't expect to get them cheap. They involve the tyer in a lot more time and trouble than ordinary patterns and you must expect to pay accordingly. When you come in with eight fat trout you won't begrudge the extra cost.

I shall always remember the chap who offered me a pound for one, after seeing me catch several good fish on the pattern. Three days later he was complaining bitterly because a tackle shop quoted him 25p each for copies. You'll have to pay even more than that now!

My last dry fly for stillwaters is far from being an everyday pattern but when it is 'on', it's a really deadly killer. It's the Drone, or Hover fly. On some waters you never see it, and even where it is found, seasons may pass without it appearing in sufficient numbers to attract trout:

Hook, No 10 or 12

Body, yellow-dyed ostrich herl, ribbed with black ostrich herl to imitate the wasp-like abdomen

Wing, a bunch of dun cock-hackle fibres or a pair of hackle points

Hackle, ginger cock

Use scarlet tying silk and let it show prominently at the head, or tie in a little tuft of scarlet floss.

You can fish this one wet or dry; if dry, don't drag it. Let it sit. The late Cyril Inwood was, I think, the first to draw attention to the effectiveness of the Drone, and since then I've always carried half a dozen in my box, because I know the day will come when no other pattern will be nearly so good. I've already had a few such days.

There you are, then; some dry flies that I always keep in my box because so very often they catch better than any wet fly.

PART THREE
Tactics

How To Cast

The question of instruction in angling has been much discussed in recent years, and of all its aspects that of fly-casting instruction has attracted most attention. This may be due to the very considerable expansion in trout-fishing, brought about by the construction of many large water-supply reservoirs, stocked with trout, and, more recently, the acceptance of more rods on some of our rivers.

In consequence, there are more people of all ages wishing to learn to cast a fly now than ever before. Most of them teach themselves, by reading advice or watching other anglers, or both. Some seek professional tuition, others are taught by amateurs. The result is an average casting standard that is very low indeed, not surprising when one considers that much of the teaching is not only incorrect, but such that it will prevent the pupil from ever learning to cast properly, unless he learns to forget it.

From time to time I am asked to teach people to cast and when I can find time, I accept these invitations. Time and again, the pupils tell me about previous instruction they have had. 'I say, Sir!' pipes a youngster, 'my pater tells me to keep my wrist stiff!'

'Brigadier X made me keep my elbow close to my side.'

'Mr Y made me push the rod-butt up my sleeve.'

'I say, Sir, my uncle says I must always stand right foot forward.'

'My last instructor said the rod should never go back past the vertical. And he made me keep my thumb on top of the rod-butt!'

These unfortunate people seem to have absorbed any amount of very bad advice, and someone must have provided it. I fear that with the best intentions, there are people taking it upon themselves to instruct in fly casting who do not know how to cast a fly correctly and, in many cases, know nothing about the art of instruction either, since a great deal of their advice begins with the word 'don't'.

Words are no substitute for proper personal instruction, but if I describe the action of correct casting with a single-handed fly rod, it may help to make some of our incompetent instructors think a little.

Stand with your left foot forward, if you are right-handed, as you would stand to serve at tennis, or draw a longbow. When you become skilled, you may cast seated or kneeling, but stand as I have advised when you are learning.

103

This is an 'open' stance that allows the use of all the muscles, and it also allows you to turn your head to watch your back-cast. If you stand right foot forward, you cannot do that, unless you are an owl.

Hold the rod with whatever grip feels most comfortable. Most people find that the thumb lies halfway between the inner side of the grip and the top of it. All four fingers are wrapped round the grip. Extend 10 yd of line in front. You can get a friend to pull it out, or extend it by walking backwards.

With your arm extended well in front, horizontal but not stretched, and the rod horizontal, too, begin the back-cast by tilting the wrist, slowly raising the rod until it makes an angle of about 75 degrees to the horizontal. Your right hand should be at the same height above the ground as your ears.

Bring your hand back and across the body quite quickly, in a straight horizontal line, as if you were pulling a drawer from a chest of drawers at eye level. When the right hand is as far back as it can comfortably go, tilt the wrist back, so that the rod butt moves through about 30 degrees, from being tilted forwards to being tilted back.

At the same time turn the head to watch the back-cast, which should extend horizontally. When it has come within about 80 per cent of becoming straight, bring the right hand forwards, quite fast, in a straight line, past your ear and forwards as far as you can reach without stretching. At the end of this movement, tilt the wrist forwards through about 30 degrees. That's the forward-cast. Take care to keep the reel in the same plane throughout; don't let it turn in relation the movement of the right hand.

All the time this is happening, the line between butt ring and reel is held in the left hand. Each time the right wrist is tilted, either backwards or forwards, the left hand pulls some line through the butt ring, and then feeds it back through the ring as the line extends. In the final forward-cast, the left hand releases the line.

How much line the left hand pulls depends on how far you are trying to cast; for long-range work it may pull as much as 5 ft.

That is basic single-handed fly casting, for distance. You don't always need distance, but it pays to learn the distance style at the beginning, because once it is learned, you can always use less of it. For shorter throws, you can use a smaller linear movement of the right hand, a smaller wrist tilt, a shorter pull of the left hand on the line. For modest distances, some of these movements will be almost imperceptible; but it is important that they are all there, because that makes for effortless, fatigue-free casting. Everything is under better control; and that, in turn, improves accuracy and delicacy. It also makes casting into a brisk breeze perfectly easy.

Detecting Takes

Since the considerable expansion in stillwater fly-fishing that began in the 1960s, a great deal has been written about the detection of takes when fishing sunk flies of imitative kinds and especially imitations of nymphs, midge and sedge pupae. We are constantly told that great numbers of trout are constantly taking and ejecting our flies without our knowing anything about it, but that with the aid of white or peach-coloured fly-lines, or partly greased leaders, plus eyes like those of a peregrine falcon, we may hope to hook a higher proportion of these taking fish.

That there are circumstances in which trout in still waters do take and eject artificial flies without giving the angler any indication I accept, but I believe they are much less frequently encountered than is commonly supposed, and that when they do occur, very often it is the kind of artificial chosen, the method of fishing it, or the choice of line and leader that are partly or wholly responsible.

To begin with, when a trout takes any item of natural food, except molluscs, crustacea, and beetles or beetle-like creatures such as corixae, it expects to find something soft in its mouth. Consequently, imitations of pupae and nymphs are less likely to be rejected rapidly if they are made of soft materials; bodies of feather fibre, fur, hair or wool, rather than floss or one of the modern hard synthetic materials. I sometimes catch trout by allowing a fly to lie entirely inert on the bottom; fish come along, pick it up and swim away with it, not infrequently running line off the reel. There is no hint of rapid rejection here; but the flies I use for that sort of static fishing are tied with rather fat herl or wool bodies, or in one instance, fairly soft expanded polyethylene. These latter patterns imitate small fish and they feel like small fish, too.

Next, we are frequently told that nymph and pupa imitations should be fished very slowly, or simply allowed to hang suspended

105

beneath the surface, usually aided by a greased leader, and only twitched by a fraction of an inch now and then. In the first place, an artificial so fished will have a good deal of slack leader and line between it and the angler. It may be cast dead straight, though that is rare, but even if it is, the effect of wind, drift and thermal currents of water will put bends and curves in it. In these circumstances the angler is forced to rely on a visual indication of a take; he cannot feel it.

Why are we advised to fish these patterns inert or only slowly? Their natural prototypes are far from slow. An ephemerid nymph or a sedge pupa coming up to hatch moves quite rapidly; it must do so in order to break through the surface film. Midge pupae (chironomids) do hang below the surface film, motionless for long periods, but they must descend 6 in or more in order to rise again at speed and break through the film. Furthermore, at the least disturbance, they go wriggling wildly down, sometimes several feet. Collect some in a bucket of water and experiment; you will soon discover what they do and how fast they can move. I think it extremely likely that when they are hanging below the surface film, they can detect the approach of a trout before it reaches them, and go wriggling away in a general downward direction. When you see trout eating midge pupae, you observe that while they break water with dorsal fins and upper tail-lobes, they seldom do so with their mouths. They are eating pupae wriggling about a few inches below the surface, not hanging inert in the surface film.

I therefore fish nymphs and pupae much faster than I am advised by other anglers to fish them. I do not mean that these patterns are stripped through the water as fast as lures often are; but I keep them on the move, and that means that I am in touch all the time and can feel at once if the fly is taken.

Why does a trout reject an artificial? If it feels wrong in his mouth, or if he is already suspicious before he takes it. One thing that may make him suspicious is a greased leader floating on the surface, specially in sunshine. I take care to avoid having any of my leader floating, thereby eliminating one cause for suspicion on the part of the trout. An inert floating leader is bad enough; a moving one is a good deal worse and as I have explained, I keep my fly moving and that means moving the leader, which must therefore be sunk.

Even the wake produced by knots in the leader may sometimes alarm trout. I use knotless tapered leaders all the time. For economy's sake, I often use a level extension at the point, when the knotless taper has been shortened by fly-changing, but if I suspect that the knot by which this extension is attached may be putting fish off, I replace the whole leader by a new knotless one. That trout are aware of leader knots, I have no doubt; I have seen trout actually take leader knots into their mouths too many times to think otherwise.

We have also to consider the effect of the line. Regular readers will know how strongly I deprecate white or pale fly-lines, which flash in sunshine, are easily visible in the air against dark backgrounds, and are very obtrusive when on the water outside the trout's window. Now, the only thing I have ever heard argued in favour of these light-coloured lines is that they are easier for the angler to see. It happens that I can see a dark line as far as I can throw it, and I can see it much more easily on a light-reflecting surface than a white line; but let us concede that most anglers can see a white line more easily, or say they can.

The method I use to fish nymphs and pupae makes it quite unnecessary to see the line. I can feel the take, and because I use soft materials in my fly patterns, the trout hold on to them longer, so that even if the take occurs in a pause between pulls, the next, immediate, pull meets resistance, signifying that the fly has been taken. That interval between retrieve-pulls is much too short to allow any slackness in the line or leader to develop.

There are conditions in which the amount of pulling that needs to be done is less; this is when the wind acting on the floating line helps to keep the fly moving. However, although the line is then in a curve, it is in constant tension, as any angler can discover if he pulls extra line or backing from the reel and releases it. The wind will promptly draw it through the rod-rings. Consequently, with the line under tension in this way, takes are felt as well as if the angler were retrieving.

It is true that the natural movements of nymphs and pupae are mainly in a vertical plane, whereas the movements of an artificial pulled by the angler, or the wind, or a combination of both, are mainly horizontal. The trout do not seem to mind this, and are as willing to take a horizontally moving fly as a vertically moving one. When they do, you know all about it without having to watch a greased leader or a pale-coloured fly-line!

107

Big Reservoirs

I do not know how often George Roberts fishes large reservoirs like Grafham and Rutland, but in his article 'The Food Factor in Fly-fishing' he gives the impression that waters of this sort are devoid of surface insects, and that the normal practice is, as he puts it, 'to attach a random succession of lunatic confections reminiscent of nothing in nature, hurl them out on a lead-core line, sink them *in profundis*, then twitch them back in the hope that one of them excites an acceptance'.

It is quite true that this practice has little or nothing to do with the kind of fly-fishing that developed on rivers generally and chalk streams in particular; but in the first place, there is a great deal more to fishing deep lures than Mr Roberts appears to think, and in the second place, it is unusual to find the conditions on a large reservoir such that deep lure fishing is either necessary or desirable.

For at least part of most days, there will be surface food for the trout somewhere, and at some time, on these reservoirs, and the angler who prefers, as I do, to catch trout with a floating line and a single, insect-imitating fly, will be unfortunate indeed if he fails to find the opportunity to do so. Indeed, there are many days when one can use a floating fly to deadly effect, notwithstanding advice to the contrary that appears in more than one book devoted to stillwater fly-fishing.

At the very beginning of the trout-fishing season, huge hatches of black midges occur on most lowland reservoirs. Popular opinion has it that at this time the deep-sunk lure is essential. Popular opinion is mistaken. At such times the deep-sunk lure catches mainly blackish rainbow trout, either heavy in spawn or, if they have succeeded in shedding their spawn, emaciated, unfit to eat and unable to fight. Anglers who know better fish an imitation of the black midge pupa and catch clean fish, smaller perhaps but in excellent condition.

As the season progresses, the variety of midges, in size and colour, increases and there are few days when none are in evidence. More often, several kinds are present and it often happens that trout feed

108

selectively on only one kind, so that the angler has to discover which this is and select an effective imitation.

By June, sedges of various kinds start to appear and imitations of their pupae and of the newly hatched fly will score. Again, the pupae vary in colour and it often happens that selective feeding occurs, so that the angler has to fish the correct imitation.

In July, various terrestrial animals are usually evident. They include hover, or drone, flies, flying ants, and in recent years quite large numbers of both ladybirds and small black beetles of similar size. On some of the older reservoirs, ephemerid species are also found from May onwards, usually pond and lake olives. At Darwell, I have collected on the same day pond olives, lake olives, the so-called summer mayfly (*Siphlonurus armatus*) the common mayfly (*Ephemera danica*) and caenis, and caught trout with imitations of all of them except *Siphlonurus*.

Sometimes as early as August, by which time sedge flies are usually present in large numbers, another chance to catch trout, often very big trout, on the dry fly occurs, when daddy-long-legs are blown onto the water. These continue to appear until the trout-fishing season ends, and once there has been enough all at once to interest the fish, the artificial daddy, if correctly tied and fished, will bring up trout even on those days when the naturals fail to appear.

There are thus opportunities to catch trout on imitative artificial flies fished either floating or just below the surface on most days, or at least during part of most days; and even when these opportunities are not present, it is seldom necessary to turn to deeply sunk lures. Instead, weighted imitative patterns like corixae, damsel and dragonfly nymphs, shrimps, hog-louse and others may be fished deeply on a long leader and floating line. It is less satisfying than surface fishing, but nearer to real fly-fishing than using sinking lines and tandem lures.

At any time, traditional loch-style fishing may be tried if a boat is available. This involves settling the boat crosswind and drifting, usually with a drogue, while the anglers cast a short line bearing a team of flies ahead of the drifting boat. For myself, I find this almost as dreary and mechanical as fishing a sunk lure, but there is no denying that it is usually effective, as the results of fly-fishing matches, often fished on unpropitious days, clearly show. It involves a great deal more skill and knowledge than may appear at first sight.

So does fishing the deep lure, in which the angler who fishes 'a random succession of lunatic confections' and does no more than chuck them out on a lead-cored line and twitch them back, will account for relatively few fish. It is necessary to know where to fish, how deep to fish, and how to ensure that the lure fishes at the correct depth, all of which requires knowledge, judgement and skill. In addition, it may be necessary to discover what deep-lying trout are eating and to fish the appropriate lure. When, for example, the trout are eating perch fry 30 ft down, a tandem lure that incorporates the features whereby trout recognise little perch will prove much more effective than any 'lunatic confection'.

As I have said, this is not a method of fishing that appeals much to me or to many others, but I have practised it, and seen it practised, enough to know that it can separate good anglers from boneheads as effectively as dry-fly or nymph-fishing can.

I would add that no one need fear that this method of fishing lures on fast-sinking or lead-cored lines will spread to other waters than large reservoirs, for the best of reasons, which is that it is useless elsewhere. Weed and lack of depth ensure that on rivers and small lakes.

Even on the large waters where it can be used to good effect, it catches few fish that might otherwise fall to surface methods. I am well convinced that when stock fish are released in large reservoirs, they soon sort themselves out into distinct categories, some adopting predominantly surface or near-surface feeding habits, others seeking food from weed-beds or dam walls, yet others exploiting the food potential of the deeper areas. Some of these groups even vary in appearance. Surface-feeding brown trout are often as silvery and as free from red spots as fresh-run sea trout, while the big browns that are encountered deep down are usually heavily spotted with both black and red spots, and have cream or even bright yellow bellies, with golden scales.

The deep-lure method therefore catches mostly trout that would not otherwise be caught at all. It is as legitimate as trolling for ferox in a Scottish loch, and perhaps almost as dreary – until one hooks a trout that may weigh 10 lb or more.

To sum up, deep-lure fishing is hardly ever the only way to catch reservoir trout; it will not spread to other waters because it fails on those; it demands skill, knowledge and judgement to be effective where it is suitable; and it catches few fish that might have been taken with surface or near-surface methods, for which there are plenty of opportunities to use on most days.

Nymph-fishing on Running Waters

To present a dry fly to a rising fish so that the fly comes down the current ahead of the leader (cast), you throw across stream, above and beyond the fish, and then mend upstream with enough force to draw the fly towards you, in line with the fish, and at the same time put an upstream loop in the line.

By this means, not only does the fly arrive at the fish with the nylon leader upstream of it, but drag is largely eliminated because the upstream bow thrown into the line must, except perhaps where there are large eddies and cross-currents, straighten out and then recurve downstream before the fly can drag.

So much we can read in Reg Righyni's book *Grayling*, published by Macdonalds and reissued in 1996 by Swan Hill Press. Exactly the same technique can be applied to a sinking nymph.

Those excellent books about nymph-fishing written, respectively, by Frank Sawyer and the late Oliver Kite, set out in detail the techniques for catching trout and grayling by casting a weighted nymph upstream. As far as it goes, the advice is sound; but it is applicable mainly to catching trout, during the time of year when trout fishing is possible. At that time, both trout and grayling are to be found mainly in shallow water, and the latter species, even when in deeper water, is willing to come up for a fly or nymph.

In autumn and winter this is not always so. In many rivers, the grayling are in the deeper holes which, in most cases, cannot easily be reached with a directly upstream cast. Even those that can do not always respond to the standard upstream techniques, because directly the line falls on the water, it becomes subject to current drag which prevents even a leaded nymph from sinking to deep-lying fish. It may go down 3 ft or so, which is well enough in summer, but not enough when grayling are hugging the bottom of a 6- or 7-ft midstream hole in November or December.

Reg Righyni's technique for the dry fly can be used as a remedy. The dry fly is replaced by a quick-sinking nymph, with either lead or copper wire in its dressing. From the time the upstream mend is made,

111

the nymph sinks freely until the current has taken the floating fly-line past it, and a downstream curve begins to form instead. By that time, the nymph has sunk deep and, if the angler has judged his distances and dimensions correctly, it is somewhere quite near the bottom, in front of the noses of the grayling.

The current, taking charge of the fly-line, now produces a pull on the nymph, causing it to rise, and it takes a course very similar to that of a nymph cast upstream and then pulled by the angler to provoke what Oliver Kite called an 'induced take'. The difference is that the angler doesn't have to do it; the current does it for him. All he has to do is watch the fly-line for a check, and tighten firmly when he sees one. The only exception is in very slow glides, where it sometimes pays to accelerate the nymph, once the downstream curve in the line begins to form, by raising the rod. Sometimes it is better to do this steadily; sometimes a series of little jerks seems to attract grayling better.

This technique can be remarkably effective, and it does enable grayling to be caught in good numbers at times when no other method of fly-fishing works, and one's thoughts turn to trotting tackle, float, shot and gilt-tail worms. In so far as such methods are not permitted on many waters holding grayling, the 'mended nymph' system has its advantage. I must emphasise that this technique is quite different from conventional downstream wet-fly fishing, in which line-drag commences almost immediately the line is on the water, and the track of the fly is across the current at approximately constant depth. Whether the objections to this style are valid or not, they do not apply to the 'mended nymph', which descends to near the bottom and then rises again, following a track almost identical to that taken by a nymph fished upstream in the ordinary way, but able to go deeper where that is desirable.

The actual depth to which the nymph will go depends upon how it is weighted, as with copper or lead wire, how large an upstream mend the angler makes, and the speed of the current. Making the upstream mend is not difficult, except in a very strong downstream wind, but where to lay the line, how far to cast across, how much to mend and from where to cast relative to the position of the fish, are matters calling for nice judgement. I have no doubt that the method can be applied to catching trout, but it is for autumn grayling that I have used it myself, and very effective it is.

Feeling for the Fish

It does not take many visits to stillwater trout fisheries to bring a fly-fisher the experience of having a fish follow a fly that he is retrieving. Sometimes the fish itself can be seen; more often one sees a bow-wave.

The problem is what to do in these circumstances. With a sunk fly it is impossible to see whether the fish has taken the fly or not, or to tell if the fly is in the mouth of the fish, whether the fish has closed its mouth.

Of one thing I am sure, and that is that if the angler continues to retrieve at the same steady pace, his chances of hooking the fish are small. What usually happens is that the fish follows the fly, or perhaps continues on the same course with the fly in its mouth, at the same speed, until it comes close enough to the angler to see him, whereupon it sheers off. If in fact it takes the fly, the angler will not know that has happened, if he continues a steady retrieve. The fish will discover the artificiality of what it has taken, and eject it.

It is significant that successful hooking of following fish often occurs when the angler attempts to lift his line from the water. I am not sure whether this is due to the trout seeing an acceleration of the fly, which stimulates it to take, or whether the attempted lift-off connects with the fish that already has the fly in its mouth; but the fact that the attempt to lift off does so often connect may give the clue to the best course of action when a trout is seen to be following the fly, or at any rate when one appears to be doing so.

The method consists in ceasing the retrieve momentarily, and then, by raising the rod as well as drawing line through the rings, to accelerate the fly smoothly and at an increasing rate, in much the same way as one would use to lift the line from the water.

The difference between the action used and the normal lift-off is that a longer, smoother and somewhat slower pull is applied, the angler 'feeling for the fish' all the time. More often than not, the fish will indeed be felt and the drawing action can then be changed to a smooth, positive tightening to set the hook.

113

The advantage of this procedure is that it matters not whether the trout has actually taken the fly or not; if it has, the increase in the speed of the fly will tighten the line, which the angler will feel. If it hasn't, the acceleration of the fly may induce a take, which the angler will also feel quite positively.

Since I adopted this technique for following fish, I have hooked a far higher percentage of them. I am inclined to think that more often than not it is a case of the acceleration of the fly inducing a take, because I have also succeeded with a similar technique when casting across the wind to fish that are moving upwind.

When the course of such fish can be observed and their speed assessed, it is possible to cast well ahead of a fish and a yard or so beyond his line. If at the point where the angler judges that the fish is near the fly the same accelerative motion is applied as I have described for following fish, a very positive take is very often induced. Indeed, it is often a very savage take, with a risk of breakage if one is fishing a fine leader point. This is why it is of advantage to apply the acceleration not only by pulling line through the rings, but also by raising the rod. The take then comes when the rod is well up, and is better cushioned.

This method works successfully even with fly patterns that imitate insects and other creatures that are quite incapable of movement at a pace anything like that imparted by the angler to his artificial. It even works with imitations of midge pupae.

There is, of course, nothing new in the idea of the induced take, though in the case of many patterns of wet fly, there may be more in it than movement. I have carried out some experiments involving a fat perspex tube with a current of water flowing through it, inside which a fly can be placed, so as to allow observation of how it reacts to variations in flow rate. In other words, it is possible to see how its appearance varies with different retrieve rates, at least to some extent.

These experiments indicate a considerable variation in the appearance of conventional wet flies, things like Peter Ross, Dunkeld, Butcher and so on, as their speed through water is varied. As a generalisation, it can be said that the faster they move, the more like a small fish they look.

Even dressings like Red Tags and other hackle flies look remarkably fishy when pulled really quickly; at any rate they do inside the perspex tube when the tap is turned on.

What the experiment fails to show is the effect of a jerky retrieve, with the feathers opening and shutting. This has always been held to be attractive to fish, but I am inclined to doubt whether it actually is. It seems more likely that flies of this kind have an optimum retrieve speed, giving the most attractive shape. After all, the number of fish that take a fly that is being retrieved – to change it – by winding the reel would indicate something of the sort. Remember, I am talking about conventional wet flies of conventional shape.

It therefore appears to me that smooth acceleration of some flies may not only attract trout to take through the movement alone, but also by the assumption by the fly of a more attractive shape at the same time.

Any fly is seen by a following trout from its rear, whereas when we dress it, and when we examine natural insects that we try to make our artificials resemble, we tend to look at both in side elevation. If one looks at a fly from the rear, one is inclined to wonder why a trout should take it at all. Perhaps more attention to how a wet fly looks to a trout following it might result in increased effectiveness.

Caenis-hatch Tactics

Fishing is full of frustrations, but I can think of nothing more frustrating than watching trout of all sizes gorging themselves on caenis, knowing that in these circumstances they are all but impossible to catch. Indeed, catching trout when they are so occupied is as difficult as it is to discover how the name of their diet is pronounced. I have heard the word 'caenis' pronounced in as many ways as Facey Romford's dupes suggested for spelling the word 'cat'.

It is not very difficult to devise what looks like a good imitation of a caenis. One has ample opportunity to observe the natural, which alights in hundreds on one's clothes, hat, glasses, rod, fishing bag and car, where it proceeds to perform a striptease act worthy of a Soho club. I have long since lost count of the different attempts I have made to imitate this insect. I have used all sorts of materials for body, thorax and wings, without ever producing a pattern that has accounted for more than an odd fish. At a guess, I would say that for every fish that I have caught on the artificial, about fifty have ignored it.

115

Brian Clarke suggests in his book *The Pursuit of Stillwater Trout* that the fish cannot actually see the insects they are eating, but simply swim where these flies are thickest on the water, with their mouths open. This may well be the case, and if so, it would account for the occasional success of the artificial which, if placed in the path of a trout, may be taken fortuitously. In that case, practically any pattern so placed would do as well, and I suspect that this sometimes happens.

Unfortunately, it cannot be used as a deliberate tactic with much hope of success, because the big hatches of caenis always occur on warm, calm evenings and the movements of trout in these conditions are entirely unpredictable. Selective feeding by trout on most other insects is either accompanied by an upwind movement of the fish, even in the slightest breeze, or the insects involved sit on the surface and are taken by trout swimming a foot or so down and rising to insects they can see, as in the case of mayflies, pond and lake olives, crane-flies and the various sedges. No such things happen with caenis.

What, then, can the angler do when he is faced with dozens of trout in easy casting distance, all busy gobbling caenis?

I have two patterns that cannot fairly be called successful: only less unsuccessful than others. They are based on two theories. One was put forward by David Jacques, who has suggested that provided the colours of a sunk fly are right, the trout will usually accept an imitation that is larger than the natural insect. The other is a notion of my own, that given the right colours, their distribution is not very important. One of my patterns is a small Chomper, with a white ostrich-herl body and a straw-coloured Raffene back, a very simple thing to tie. I carry this in sizes 12 and 14, fish it on a 3-lb b.s. point, and it often accounts for a brace of fish in a caenis hatch. I fish it on a floating line and a degreased, sinking leader, and pull it fast enough to keep it within an inch or two of the surface.

The other fly is tied on a No 12 long-shank hook, and consists of three swan-herl bodies of equal length and four cream cock-hackles tied in series along the shank. Sepia tying silk is used and allowed to show at the roots of each hackle. The idea is to offer three or four, as you wish, caenis for the price of one, so to speak. This fly is called the Lucky Alphonse, and it can either be fished dry and motionless, or allowed to sink and moved very slowly. It, too, has often managed a brace of fish in a caenis hatch, but I hasten to add that for every fish it has caught, dozens have refused or ignored it.

116

The difficulty of catching trout when they are eating caenis lies not only in the behaviour of the fish in relation to artificial flies, but also in the ease with which one can alarm them by inadvertently dropping the fly-line on their heads. They seem largely oblivious to the presence of the angler on the bank but acutely conscious of the fall of the fly-line, be it ever so delicately cast. Indeed, continuous casting will rapidly clear the area within casting range of fish, though plenty can be seen feeding industriously just out of range. Move to cover them, and within a few minutes they will be busy in the area you have just vacated.

It helps to use a little soft-actioned rod, a very light fly-line, and to cast always to the nearest fish, which is often very near indeed, which is why you need a soft rod capable of handling a short length of light line. I do not find a very long leader advantageous, because it prevents really accurate casting. Ten feet is ample and I usually use a leader of 8 or 9 ft.

Caenis hatches almost always occur in the evening, and fortunately for the angler, they sometimes peter out at the edge of dusk and are succeeded by a hatch of sedges. One has to be alert for this, or opportunities will be missed. The change from eating caenis to eating sedges is indicated by splashing rises, or even leaps by the trout, instead of the sipping and gobbling rises that signify caenis-eating. It pays to take the extra time needed to change to a stronger leader point when switching to the artificial sedge, because a floating sedge is often taken with considerable violence and it is all too easy to be broken, even when tightening gently, if the fine point suitable for the caenis hatch is retained.

As well as trying to incorporate the assumed recognition points of the winged caenis in artificial flies, I have also tried to imitate the nymph, with indifferent success. The pattern with which I have done best, admittedly a poor best, has short cream cock-hackle tails, an abdomen of short-fibred cream ostrich herl, natural black feather-fibre abdomen, cock blackbird wing-cases and legs, and is tied on a No 16 hook. This sometimes catches a trout before the hatch commences in earnest. I tie it on directly I see a single winged caenis, but once the hatch commences in earnest, it becomes virtually useless.

For some unexplained reason, not all the trout in a lake take advantage of caenis hatches. I have often watched fish, in clear water, cruising about, apparently oblivious of the activities of their fellows at the surface. If one is anxious to catch a few fish, rather than persevere with the problem of catching those that are eating caenis, it is probably better to fish a pattern that bears no resemblance to caenis, and to fish it at midwater or near the bottom. A few days ago, I watched a big brown trout busily eating cased caddis at the bottom of a shallow area, while large numbers of fish were busily gobbling caenis nearby, and this was by no means the only trout I saw that had no interest in the caenis hatch. It depends upon what one regards as the object of one's operation: trying to solve the problem of caenis-eating trout, or making a respectable bag. Regrettably, the former seldom, if ever, leads to the latter.

Wading

One of our most thoughtful writers about trout fishing, Peter Lapsley, drew attention recently to the effects of wading in trout lakes and reservoirs. I was rather slow to accept some of the points he made, but on reflection I think he was right in suggesting that, in general, wading is disadvantageous on waters of that kind.

One of the waters I fish regularly is a 15-acre lake in Bedfordshire, the hole from which gravel was excavated having been nicely land-scaped. It produces a wide variety of insects but its special feature is sedge hatches, which start in late May and go on till the end of the season. Most of these are fairly small brown jobs, imitated on a No 12 hook, but at times there are the bigger cinnamon sedges, and very occasionally the outsize one, the great red sedge, *Phryganea grandis*.

Hatching often takes place well out from the bank and long casting is then necessary, but there are always lots of these insects flitting about around the margins or sitting on the stalks of rush grass. You can knock them up with a landing net handle on the weather shore, when some fall in and induce a local rise. Their caddises are easily visible in the water close to the bank, specially those of the cinnamon sedges.

Consequently, when these various kinds of sedge are flying about, you can usually catch some trout either by what Skues called the cross-country cast, or by casting along the margins, dropping the fly no more than a yard out and often much less.

Wading is not allowed. I am perfectly sure that if it were, quite serious damage would be done to the sedge-fly population, and even if enough sedges remained to attract trout close inshore, they would be driven out by wading anglers.

At Two Lakes, where wading is also *verboten*, the quantity of nymphs, caddis and snails that can be seen within a yard of the bank is huge. The same may be said of such areas of most water-supply reservoirs as are set aside as nature reserves or bird sanctuaries. The water close to the bank is alive with potential trout food, and anglers, by wading, are in effect driving trout into areas where they cannot fish for them. We all know that there always seems to be far more trout in those areas; it is no illusion. There are more trout there because there is more food by far and no fish-scaring wading anglers.

It is sometimes amazing to see anglers wading where the slope of the bank is so steep that they can advance no more than a yard or two from the bank. Wading has for them become a habit. I remember fishing at Grafham with Peter Thomas some years ago, from the bank of Savage's Creek. We had a long walk from the car, not made more pleasant by wearing thigh waders. Having arrived at our chosen spot, we started to wade out, only to find that a combination of steep slope and soft mud limited us to 5 or 6 ft from dry land. After a few casts Peter said, 'Why are we wading? We could cast farther standing on dry land!' So we could, and did, catching a lot of fish, including some four-pounders. We did not, in fact, need to cast more than about 15 yd to catch them.

At Draycote, Peter and I were once driving slowly along the perimeter road when we spotted numbers of fish rising very close to the bank. We went down, and casting from a good 10 yd back from the water's edge we caught a couple of fair fish each; then another car stopped and three anglers emerged, marching straight down the bank and into the water, where they waded out as far as their thighboots permitted. All activity by the trout ceased and Peter and I moved to another area.

Examination of the bottom of most reservoirs will reveal that wherever wading is allowed, by the end of May it has become impossible to wade without treading in a previously made foot-print. Every form of aquatic life has been trampled out of existence, as far out as thigh waders allow anglers to paddle.

The loss of fish food is incalculable. With the exception of many species of midge and of such planktonic animals as daphnia, most

119

aquatic species live in relatively shallow water, where light can penetrate to the bottom, and it is these very areas where wading does most damage.

It is true that in most large reservoirs, midge pupae and daphnia appear to constitute the greater part of the diet of the trout, but we learn this from autopsies, which might tell a somewhat different story if other potential food forms were permitted to proliferate.

When reservoirs are first opened, it is common to find huge populations of sedges and sticklebacks. After the first season, stickle-backs almost disappear and sedges become fewer. That has happened on every new reservoir that I have fished, and it is at least possible that mass wading is responsible. Stickleback nests are seldom found in water more than 2 ft deep.

What are the advantages of wading? Some are undeniable. The weight carried by an angler's feet is reduced by the weight of water that his legs displace and he can go on fishing much longer without tiring if he wades. Wading also reduces his effective height, so that trout have to be nearer before they can see him.

Theoretically, he can reach greater casting distance: that is, he can place his fly farther from the bank. I think that in most cases this is an illusion. Only where the slope of the bottom is very gentle indeed can an angler wade out far enough to gain much advantage. Double-haul casting is inhibited when one wades deep, by the hauling hand hitting the water.

Quite apart from its damaging effect on potential trout food, wading has numerous disadvantages, not the least of which is the cost of waders, the discomfort of walking a long way in them, and the inevitable flooding of them that, if not encountered every time we fish, catches nearly all of us too often. Having discovered that I can catch as many fish without wading, I have now abandoned it.

There are times when numbers of other anglers are wading and one feels at a disadvantage without waders oneself; the extra mobility provided by wearing ordinary walking shoes or, in wet weather, shooting boots, usually means that a place can be found where no one is trying to trample on the trout.

Yet despite the disadvantages of wading from so many points of view, I would hesitate to advocate a total ban on big waters. Some kind of compromise might, however, be tried, consisting in setting aside fairly extensive no-wading areas, and watching these to discover if catches from them were any less, or aquatic life substantially increased. I believe some such experiment is already being carried out at Rutland and it will be interesting to hear what the findings are.

I should be surprised if catches were found greatly to increase in no-wading areas, because although more trout are likely to be found in them, I expect such trout to be harder to catch, and to need careful fishing of imitative fly patterns rather than fast-stripped large lures. With more trout that are harder to catch, the yield may be about the same from wading and non-wading areas. That should not be taken to invalidate the idea that wading is on balance harmful; even if we catch no more trout from non-wading areas, they ought to be better fed and they ought to be more interesting to catch, as well as saving us the cost of thigh boots and the discomfort of wet legs.

Tactics for High Noon

In the last two or three seasons, I have done a good deal of trout fishing on the smaller, man-made waters, where I often meet anglers who tell me how futile it is to try to catch trout in the middle hours of a sunny day, specially if the water's surface is calm.

That there are difficulties produced by such conditions I do not deny, but there is one very great advantage where most waters are concerned. The fish can be seen; and this enables the angler to cast to the bigger ones, thus greatly improving his chances of catching one or more of them.

In addition, there is often a reduction in activity by other anglers about midday. Many, having flogged away to no purpose for several hours in the morning, go away, eat their lunch (or drink it) and then laze about until late afternoon, thinking the chances of fish will remain poor until then.

As one of the greatest handicaps to catching fish, specially big fish, on these waters is the activity of other anglers, from midday until perhaps 4 p.m. is often a good time to fish, even in calm, bright conditions. The ingredients of success can be partly deduced by observing what these unsuccessful anglers commonly do.

They wander about the banks, bolt upright. They are unanimous in their choice of white or pale-coloured fly-lines. They seldom take steps to ensure their leaders are free from glint and that they sink directly they touch the water; indeed it is not at all uncommon to find them greasing leaders to make them float.

They cast standing up, and each cast is preceded by several false-casts. By the time the line is on the water, any trout in the vicinity will have left it in terror, if they have not already done so through having seen the arrival of the angler or felt the vibrations of his tread as he clumped along the bank.

The older I grow, the more I realise the value of some advice I had from my grandfather when I was seven or eight years old. 'Pretend every fish has a gun,' he said, 'and if it sees you, it'll shoot you dead!'

The way to catch fish in bright, calm weather is to go looking for them, dressed drably, moving slowly and quietly, and treading softly. Much depends on bank-side cover, but there are few lakes where there is none, and it is usually possible to move from one piece of cover to another by making a detour, well back from the water's edge. The background should be watched, so as to avoid as far as possible becoming silhouetted against the sky. So also should the angle of the sun, to ensure that the shadow of the line, the rod and the angler himself does not frighten the trout.

Rods new-bought are covered with shiny varnish. Professional rod-makers all know that this frightens fish, but it attracts customers; there is virtually no sale for rods finished matt. It is, however, easy to remove the shine from varnish by rubbing the rod down with a mixture of raw linseed oil and scouring (pumice) powder, applied with a soft rag. After the flash is gone, the rod is cleaned with a soft rag barely moistened with clean linseed oil.

Floating lines can be bought in a so-called mahogany colour, which is satisfactory. Any angler having a white or pale-coloured line can easily dye it in Dylon dye, mixed double strength, boiled, and allowed to cool for 15–20 minutes before the line is immersed. Let the line soak for about four hours, keeping it below the surface with a weight of some kind – a jam jar filled with water does very well. Finally, rinse the line, rub it down with a damp, soft rag and let it dry.

If touching turns have left undyed spots, uncoil the line, re-coil it and repeat the process. I find that black dye produces a very good dark sepia colour.

Leaders should be rubbed down with a mixture of fuller's earth and washing-up liquid, neat, mixed to the consistency of putty.

That famous American angler Edward Hewitt always advocated staining gut leaders dead black, with silver nitrate, for use in sunshine. Unfortunately, silver nitrate does not stain nylon black; the best one can do is to obtain a deep chestnut colour. I have done no better, so far, with black dye, but Anglers Masterline sell excellent black monofil for backing shooting heads, so perhaps they may be able to tell us how to dye knotless tapered leaders the same colour.

In the meantime, ordinary leaders dulled with the fuller's earth mixture do very well.

Of one thing I am sure, and that is that it is folly to fish too fine on these small lakes. In his book *Lake Flies and their Imitation*, Cdr C.F. Walker said something to the effect that a man who cannot land a 5-lb trout on a 16 hook and 4x point 'deserves not the name of an angler'. To judge from the flies I find beside my own in the mouths of fish I catch, there are many who are guided by the above dictum, and they lose a great many fish because of it. I seldom fish a leader finer than 2x, that is, about 6 lb dry breaking load, and more usually I use 1x, about 7 lb. I don't find that such relatively strong leaders alarm the trout, except if a very small fly has to be used; and I do not like to use smaller flies than No 12 where trout of 5 lb or more are likely to be encountered. Nor do I recommend fine-wire hooks, even for mayflies.

Among the most useful items of equipment for fishing small trout lakes are a good wide eye-shade or a broad-brimmed hat, and a pair of polarised glasses. An adequate landing net is also recommended, with a long handle.

I chuckle when I see anglers who evidently think they are dressed in the height of angling fashion: thigh waders, folding nets, tweedy hats and creels and often, American-style fishing waistcoats. I carry a folding stool and a net originally intended for coarse fishing and I wear soft shoes whenever possible. Indeed, not so long ago, an acquaintance said, 'Dick, you look like a bloody roach-fisher!' I am sure he was right, and with four trout aggregating 25 lb on the bank I felt that perhaps there is some advantage in it. I am sure that the more one moves about, the fewer trout one catches. I choose a spot, sit on my stool, and cast only when I see something at which to cast.

As many of the trout come close, if one is drably dressed and sitting still, it is often possible to present a fly without any false-casting at all. With 4 yd of fly-line beyond the tip-ring, and a 3-yd leader, the fly can be projected to a distance of nearly 10 yd by holding the fly in the left hand and switching with the rod, releasing the fly at the right moment. This is often quite far enough. I remember catching a very nice bag of fish at Damerham entirely in that way, and then being told that long-distance casting with shooting heads was unsporting and should be barred.

On big reservoirs, the ability to cast long distances can often greatly increase the catch, but on the small lakes of only a few acres, it is seldom necessary.

There can be no doubt that success on these waters depends on the realisation that they differ in many ways from either rivers or large lakes and reservoirs; and one of the most important differences is that trout may be headed in any direction. They cannot be approached from below as in river fishing, nor can they be fished for at long range, usually in a wave or ripple, as in a reservoir or loch. Therefore, stealth combined with drab dress and equipment are at a premium, and one's greatest handicap is the fellow-angler who fails to realise this.

How to Dap

Although it is allowed on some reservoirs, dapping seems never to have become popular, which is a pity, because it is an exciting as well as an effective way of catching trout.

With the rods we used to use in the 1930s, made of whole cane, about 15 ft long and rather floppy, it was also quite tiring. Now, so little dapping is done that as far as I am aware, nobody makes a rod for the purpose. Quite recently, however, I've acquired a rod which, though not made for it, will nevertheless be ideal. It's a 15-ft carbon match rod and part of its virtue is that it is very thin and doesn't catch the wind nearly as much as a cane or glass rod, an important point, since when you are out in a boat in a wind strong enough for dapping, it is wind-pressure on the rod that tires your arm and wrist.

There won't be much of that with this new carbon rod, which is also very light – no more than about 60 per cent of the weight of a glass rod of similar length and action.

In the old days we used to dap with a length of loosely plaited floss silk, which caught the wind and let you bounce your fly well out from the boat. In a good breeze this isn't necessary; you can manage with ordinary monofil, about 7-lb b.s.

If, however, you read up some of the books about big-game fishing by people like Zane Grey, Van Campen Heilner and Frederick Holder, you'll come across several mentions of a method of fishing for bluefin tuna which involved attaching a kite to the line. This enabled the angler to bounce a dead fish over the surface-feeding tuna, in a way resembling a flying fish, and it seems to have been very successful.

I should think it would be quite easy to construct a small kite, which would not need to be more than a few inches in size, to use with a dapping outfit to extend the distance that could be covered from a boat, even an anchored boat. The only real snag would be the probability that if it worked, it would soon be banned, owing to the propensity on the part of British anglers to scream for a ban on anything that turns out to be effective.

One thing I discovered early on in my experience of dapping is that you do not need natural insects. People go to considerable trouble to collect mayflies, grasshoppers or daddy-long-legs to use as dapping baits. Boxes or cow-horns to keep them in used to be sold, and there was even a special hook with a spring clip, called the 'Ayrbro', for fishing them. In fact you can do just as well with an artificial: a mayfly or daddy at appropriate times, at other times a big sedge, white moth or a muddler minnow. Artificials avoid all the time and trouble of collecting and keeping real insects, and with modern dip-in silicone-wax waterproofing liquids, they will catch several fish before needing to be changed or re-proofed.

Talking about the possibility of using a kite reminds me of another little device that ought to be more widely known – the Digby-Lancaster hatch-finder.

This consists of a small drogue, made originally of muslin, but which can now be made of nylon net-curtain material. You can make it any size you like, but a disc of 6–9 in diameter is usual. Around its circumference are attached strings – pieces of line – all joined to produce what looks like a little parachute. In its centre is a little ring to which you can tie either a wooden or a lead weight, depending on what you want to do. To the junction of the strings, you tie your line.

You may then trail the thing behind a boat, or cast it from the bank. Examination of what it has collected when you pull it in tells you which insects or other organisms are in the water, so that you can fish the appropriate imitation.

It is particularly useful when duns or midges are hatching; you can see what colour pupae or nymphs are coming up. It is quite surprising how much insect life one of these devices will collect after being pulled 20 yd or so through the water. It doesn't do so well when there is a lot of green algae in suspension; that soon clogs it up, but otherwise, it's a useful little device to have, weighing next to nothing and taking up very little room in the bag. Marrow spoons are all very well, but you have to catch a fish before you can use one. The Digby-Lancaster hatch-finder discovers what flies are about without the aid of that first fish.

Another device that can be useful where it is allowed – and you need one anyway if you're going to cast a Digby-Lancaster hatch-finder – is a wooden weight. This can be made from any heavy wood like mahogany or teak, pear-shaped with a little ring screwed into its narrow end. To this you attach the end of your line, with as many flies or droppers above it as you think fit. You cast it out, hold the rod-point high, and bob the droppers on the surface. It isn't a bubble float! Nor, despite what some may argue, is it an otter-board. The principle of an otter-board is that a pull on the line will send it planing away; it can be worked across a current to the opposite bank, or by walking along the shore of a lake, the otter-board can be run out a very long way.

The simple wooden weight does nothing of that sort. It acts as a floating anchor, to allow dropper flies to be bobbed at the surface, and since it also provides a casting weight, it allows that to be done at greater range. To use it effectively requires neither more nor less skill than is involved in traditional loch-style fishing, but I have no doubt that there are many who will say it is unsporting.

Of course, it works best in conjunction with a long coarse-fishing rod and a fixed-spool reel, but you mustn't use the latter, because as everyone knows, a fish killed on such a reel is much deader than if it had been taken on a fly reel.

It makes me chuckle when I look at the paradoxical rules that are applied. It is quite all right, it seems, to fish a real, live grasshopper on dapping tackle, but 'Dashed unsporting, what?' to fish an artificial daddy or mayfly by using a wooden casting weight – or a bubble float, which is ten times worse, killing fish ten times as dead. Yes, even when the artificial is a 'dray flay'! There are, however, waters where you are allowed to use a bit of ingenuity to have a bit of fun, and I have never known anyone who seriously reduced fish stocks by doing that.

126

Static Sunk Flies

Although the idea has been discounted by some anglers, it remains a fact that trout will sometimes pick up an artificial fly that is lying inert on the bottom of a lake or reservoir. Many anglers have discovered this by leaving line, leader and fly lying in the water while they have taken a rest or refreshment.

It would seem that when this has happened, it has usually been regarded as a freak occurrence, unlikely to be repeated. I must confess that I encountered it, now and again, over many years before I realised that, far from being abnormal, it was, in relation to the time the artificial was in the water, quite a common occurrence.

If the catch rate on a reservoir, on a favourable day, averages one fish per hour, then if a fly lying static is picked up by a trout after 20 minutes; and if this is found to happen perhaps once for every three times when the fly is allowed to lie static – which is approximately what does happen – then we must accept that taking static flies is by no means an aberrant form of behaviour by trout.

Nor is it the act of sick or out-of-condition fish, as some have suggested. I have never caught such fish on the static fly. Upon reflection, why should anyone be surprised to find trout taking inert artificial flies lying on the bottom? They very frequently take inert artificial flies floating at the surface, as everyone knows. One assumes that they do so either because they think the fly is food or because they wish to find out whether it is food or not. Exactly the same motivation would surely influence their reaction to a sunk inert fly.

However, while we know something about the most favourable circumstances for fishing inert flies on the surface, we know much less about those for fishing them at the bottom. The inert sunk fly does not always catch trout, any more than the inert floater does. Indeed, the floater succeeds better unless some thought is given to the right circumstances in which the static sunk fly can succeed.

Clearly, the first essential for any fly to be taken is to put it where the fish are. Surface-feeding trout, those likely to succumb to a static floater, are very easy to locate. Bottom feeders, likely to take the static sunk fly, are not.

I do not think many anglers would wish to set out intending to fish a static fly at the bottom as a regular practice occupying much of their fishing time. I will not deny that by comparison with conventional methods, it can be rather boring, through boredom quickly vanishes when line begins to run off the reel at a rapid pace. So, the use of the sunk static fly would normally be confined to such times as when an angler or anglers decide to consume refreshments, or simply take a rest from constant casting.

If such a break is imminent, it is worth anticipating it by choosing a suitable fly pattern and if necessary, changing to a sinking fly-line. If fishing from a boat, it is a good idea to anchor in an area where, from previous experience, it is known that insect hatches and activity by trout are both common and prolific. A depth of no more than about 12 ft is desirable, and if the bottom is clean sand or gravel, so much the better. I have caught most fish on static flies in areas which past experience has shown large numbers of good-sized sedge flies to favour – possibly because these are areas that provide not only a satisfactory food supply for their caddises but also the material for their cases.

Trout will pick up almost any size or kind of artificial fly, from small nymphs or imitations of midge pupae to large two-hook tandem lures. So the important consideration is not so much what the trout will pick up, but what the fly may pick up in the way of bottom debris or snags.

One of the most useful flies for sunk static work is a fore-and-aft pattern; a long-shank hook, about No 6 or No 8, with a stiff, long-fibred cock-hackle wound at the head, another at the start of the bend, and a body of some kind in between. I don't think it matters much what colour the body or hackles are; there isn't much in the way of colour to be seen in depths of more than 7 or 8 ft, anyway. My usual fly has white hackles and a peacock-herl body ribbed with silver tinsel.

An alternative to the fore-and-aft hackles is the use of a little lead at the back of the dressing, enough to cause the fly, whatever its pattern, to fish hook point upwards. If the body is made of several layers of floss or wool, a strip of lead foil can be tied in under the last layer. The requirement is different from that of a conventional leaded nymph or shrimp, where maximum sinking rate is wanted. For the static fly, we need a pattern as light as possible consistent with the avoidance of catching snags or rubbish, so that it does not sink into soft mud or silkweed. I would warn against keel hooks – they don't hook trout well enough.

Let's pretend that two of us are out in a boat; we have been drifting and casting for two or three hours and have taken one or two fish, but it is well past midday, our arms could do with a rest and we didn't bring the packed lunches and liquid refreshment for no reason.

Instead of simply dropping anchor where we happen to be, we motor or row to a place that we think, for various reasons, might produce a fish to a sunk static fly. We change to sinking lines – the sinking rate isn't important – and we tie suitable flies to the leaders. Only one on each. Having anchored the boat, we cast some 15 yd or so downwind, and then lay down the rods in such a way that swing by the boat on its anchor rope will not cause the lines to be pulled. We shake out a yard or two of slack to further assist in this. We also see that the rods are so placed that if a fish hooks itself, it cannot smash the rod overboard.

We sit within easy reach of the rods and, if right-handed, we use the left hand to convey food or drink to our mouths.

Not infrequently, we shall find that one of the reels will begin ticking over, or more likely screaming, long before the food and drink have been consumed. On one memorable occasion at Grafham, the static fly accounted for five trout between 2 and 3 ½ lb in under half an hour.

Fishing from the bank, one can rest the rod on a bag, but care must be taken to see that the line can run free and that the reel check is not too stiff, specially with the very light reels and rods that most of us use nowadays. I have not yet lost an entire outfit through fishing a sunk static fly, but I have come near enough to doing so to be well aware of the possibility!

Loch-style Fishing

The method of fishing from a boat that has come to be known as 'loch-style' is often very effective on lowland reservoirs, provided there is enough breeze. But it is seldom as fully exploited as it might be.

It consists essentially of casting downwind from a boat drifting broadside to the wind, whose drift rate is controlled either by a drogue or by someone using the oars. Its effectiveness depends at least partly on the fact that if more than one fly is used, the one nearest the rod can be bobbed and bounced on the surface, which is for some reason especially attractive to trout.

An examination of the forces and positions involved reveals that the time during which a dropper fly can be made to play on the surface depends on a number of factors.

These include the height of the rod point above the water, the weight of the fly-line, the angle to the wind at which the cast was made, the water resistance of the point fly and the distance between it and the dropper. The longer the rod, the lighter the line; the greater the angle of the cast to the wind direction and the greater the distance between point fly and dropper, the longer the dropper can be bobbed on the surface.

Fifty years ago, expert loch-fishers were using rods of 14 and 15 ft, double-handed. Some were even made of greenheart and must have weighed upwards of 30 ozs, yet it is evident that the advantage of length was held to be such that the weight was thought acceptable.

A few years ago I had a fibreglass rod made that was 15 ft long and weighed under 7 ozs. Casting was not tiring but holding the rod against wind pressure was. Now we have carbon-fibre, it ought to be possible to produce a rod of 12–13 ft that weighs under 5 ozs, and whose air resistance in a good breeze is acceptably low. Such a rod would offer a great advantage over the 9 and 9½-ft rods that most anglers seem to use. No great casting power is necessary; casting is all downwind and to no great distance.

The reason for favouring a light line is that between rod point and water, the line forms a catenary curve. The lighter the line, the higher is the middle of this curve above the water and consequently, the farther from the rod is the point at which the dropper fly reaches the surface when the line is tightened. However, the distance at which this occurs depends also on the water resistance of the point fly against which the line is tightened. A point fly with high water resistance will let a dropper come to the top farther away.

Obviously, the nearer the dropper is to the fly-line, the sooner it will reach the surface, but the difference made by moving it farther from the point fly and nearer the line is less than one might suppose, since once the end of the fly-line leaves the surface, the dropper rises much more rapidly because the monofil between fly-line and dropper is so light. Since the thicker fly-line may have some deterrent effect on fish, the ideal distance between fly-line and dropper becomes a matter of opinion based on experiment. I would suggest that it should be between 3 and 4 ft.

With a 12-ft rod, this permits a total leader length of about 12 ft, unless you don't mind standing up in a boat in a good wave to net a fish. I do. I don't believe that a much longer leader than about 12 ft catches more fish, but it is certainly inconvenient.

So far I have referred only to the dropper or bob fly and the point fly. An extra dropper can be placed between these two, and if the bob is 3 ft from the fly-line, this middle fly can be about 4 ft further down, which with a 12 ft leader places it 5 ft from the point fly. Unless a fish is actually seen and can be cast at, it is a good idea to cast, not directly downwind, but down and across the wind at as large an angle as can be comfortably managed. By keeping the rodpoint fairly high, the wind can be used to bow the line in the air and draw the flies at an angle across the wind, not only prolonging the time they fish, and especially the time that the bob fly works on the surface, but also drawing the flies across the tracks of feeding trout that are moving upwind. The greater the angle, within reason, that the track of the flies makes to the direction of the wind, the greater is the number of trout that will see the flies. Furthermore, many fly patterns are more attractive seen in profile than directly from the rear.

There are many differing opinions as to how multi-fly leaders should be made up, and I make no particular claim that my way is superior. However, in case any reader may wish to know about it, I will describe it. There are three lengths of monofil differing in thickness by one thousandth of an inch; usually 0.010 in next to the point fly, 0.011 in in the middle and 0.012 in between bob fly and fly-line. The two knots are Blood-Grinners with the thicker ends used to attach the flies using Grinner knots. I have one foot of 0.014 in nylon needle knotted to the end of the fly-line and the end of the leader is attached to this with a double Grinner knot. The dropper ends start at about 5 in long. A longer dropper link delays the arrival of the fly it carries at the surface. In a very strong wind, it pays to use a point fly that has not only high water resistance but also carries some lead. For some obscure reason, some fishery managements forbid the obvious course, which is to pinch a small split shot on the nylon as close as possible to the eye of the point fly, but nobody seems to mind a few layers of lead foil or turns of lead wire under the dressing.

Perhaps the greatest asset that a user of this style of fly-fishing can have is the ability to detect the presence of fish. This may be indicated by an obvious splash; by what I think of as the 'shatter' effect; by seeing a fish or the flash of one in the side of a wave; or by a small calm patch appearing at the surface. If any such indication is seen away from one's flies, they should be lifted at once and put down as quickly as possible, and as close as possible to where the sign was observed. If the sign is seen where the flies are, it is extremely likely that one has already been taken. The procedure is to avoid a sudden strike, but accelerate the drawing of the flies. If resistance is felt, the line is tightened firmly.

The surface sign means either that one of the flies has been taken, or that a fish is near. Accelerating the draw will feel the fish if it has taken, or usually induce a take if it has not.

The take to a dibbling bob fly is, of course, very obvious, but underwater takes are by no means always so, and many a fish will take and eject a fly unless a close watch of the water is constantly maintained. With a considerable curve in line and some of the leader, pulls have to be quite vehement before they are felt. Sometimes the only indication is a slight lift in the curve of line between rod and water.

It is necessary to remember that the boat is drifting towards the place where the flies alight on the water, and unless the angler draws them faster than the boat drifts, he will be out of touch and quite unable to feel a take, especially as the taking fish are mostly moving upwind towards the boat.

Drawing the flies is done by a combination of lifting the rodpoint and drawing line with the left hand. Clearly, the longer the rod, the more the flies can be drawn without using the left hand for more than a single slow pull; more than that is not recommended. That part of the pull that is made with the rod is better made at an angle to the vertical, to supplement the effect of wind on the line which, be it remembered, is cast at an angle to the direction of the wind.

With a partner at the other end of the boat, some teamwork is needed to avoid the crossing of back-casts, but if it is agreed in advance that both anglers shall cast in the same direction relative to the wind, this can be easily avoided. This may be thought to leave a strip of water unfished, but a little thought will show that there is no way of avoiding this; either you miss out a strip to one side of the line of drift, or else a strip right in the middle. To alternate casts between left and right of the wind direction is almost certain to produce crossed lines with your partner.

Fishing a Flat Calm

Flat calm conditions on lakes and reservoirs are dreaded by most trout fishers, but they do not make catching trout impossible if certain precautions are taken.

Initial observation will determine if trout are feeding at or near the surface; the angler will either be in a boat or fishing from the bank. In either case it is important to avoid surface disturbances.

The bank angler should, if possible, avoid wading. If wading is essential, he should wade with the greatest care, taking with him everything he may need, so that he need not return to the bank to change flies, to oil them, to degrease his leader, or even to dispose of any fish he may catch. The important thing is to stay still, having waded out; and to avoid producing ripples when casting.

Much the same applies when fishing from a boat. It is preferable to anchor, to move about in the boat as little as possible, and to avoid rocking the boat when casting.

When fish can be seen rising, there is always a temptation to move the boat about, seeking an area where there appear to be most fish. This is due to an optical illusion. If you look along a straight road, you will see that the telegraph poles appear to be closer and closer together, the farther they are away. For exactly the same reason, wherever you anchor your boat, you will think there are more fish rising somewhere else. If you keep rowing about, you will alarm large numbers of fish and catch few or none. So, stay anchored and wait for fish to move within range of an easy cast, a cast that demands little effort and thus avoids rocking the boat.

If trout are feeding at the surface, it will be necessary to use a floating line. To avoid wake caused by knots, it helps to use a knotless tapered leader, attached to the fly-line with a needle knot, and to degrease this leader very carefully to ensure that every inch of it sinks.

This can be done with a rag soaked in washing-up liquid, or by pulling the leader through a ball of synthetic mud made by mixing washing-up liquid, glycerine and fuller's earth to the consistency of putty. Take no notice of anything you may have been told or have read about greasing leaders to keep such patterns as midge pupae just below the surface film, or about watching the leader, duly greased, to detect a take. Always make sure that the entire leader sinks, no matter what fly you are fishing. Even if you use a dry fly, sink the leader, all of it.

If fish are seen rising out of range, do not cast at random. Extend a comfortable length of line and let it sit on the water until a rising fish comes within range. Then lift off as smoothly and with as little disturbance as possible, and re-cast to the fish.

Waiting for a fish to move into range is equally important to the bank angler when, I repeat, there is clear evidence of surface feeding. Continuous casting at random will prevent fish from moving within range.

If there is a long wait, and the line drifts too much, a careful lift-off and re-cast may be needed, causing the minimum of disturbance. The waiting period can be used for observation, to determine what insects are about and thus which artificial to choose. Naturally, when one's fly is in the water, the end of the line should be watched in case the fly, which if a wet one will have sunk several feet, is taken. You will know if a trout takes a dry fly!

If however there is no sign of surface activity by the trout, it becomes necessary to seek them at some depth. In these circumstances, an echo sounder is invaluable if you are in a boat. You can discover with its aid the depth at which most of the trout are swimming. In heatwave conditions that may be as deep as 40 ft.

With a boat, these fish can be caught; the bank angler has to wait until evening when the fish will usually come to the surface. A boat has to be anchored, and a long cast made with a high-density line; the very fast sinkers go down at about 9 in per second. The reason why a long cast is needed is that by the time the line has sunk to the correct depth, it is lying in a curve and the fly is much nearer the boat than the distance the angler has cast. On the retrieve, the fly will only fish at the correct depth for a few yards, even with a throw of 30 yd or so. With a shorter cast, it will start to come up almost as soon as the retrieve is commenced.

However, trout are only at depths of 30 or 40 ft in heatwave conditions; more commonly, if they are not at the surface they will be from 4 to 10 ft down, which puts them within reach of both boat and bank anglers. It is then a matter of searching for them, using either a floating line with a leaded fly pattern, or a slow-sinking line with a non-leaded pattern. In either case, the time allowed for the fly or the line to sink can be increased a little for every cast until either the fish are found, or the fly comes up decorated with silkweed or other evidence that it is touching bottom. When that happens, the allowance of sinking time can be reduced a little for subsequent casts and the area within range thoroughly searched.

The decision as to whether to start with a leaded fly and floating line, or sinking line and normal fly, is a matter of individual choice. My own is to start with the leaded fly on waters rich in a variety of insect life, and vice versa on waters where the production of trout food is modest, or where there is heavy stocking with trout; but if the one method fails, the other can then be tried.

Another alternative is to try a static fly on a sinking line, preferably in areas where, in the past, you have noticed sedge flies hatching in large numbers. You simply tie on a fly, cast, let everything sink to the bottom and then sit and wait for a trout to take. The most useful flies are tied with stiff cock-hackles so that they sit on the bottom without the hook catching in silkweed or debris; the Dambusters and various fore-and-aft patterns are all useful.

This may be regarded as a dreary business by many; but the dreariness ends when a fish takes, and the method does have the advantage of creating virtually no disturbance, nor is there any rod movement, after the cast is made, that can alarm trout in the area; in flat calms they can see all too easily any movement on the bank or in the boat. For the static method the boat must of course be anchored.

At Draycote, the static fly is banned, on the flimsy argument that the management cannot tell whether an angler using it has not adorned his fly with a worm or a maggot. When I first reported that a fly lying inert on the bottom would often catch trout, many readers, including anglers of long experience, expressed incredulity, some of which may still persist. I can only say that it is perfectly true, though in common with other ways of presenting a fly, it does not succeed everywhere or always.

Trout fishing in a calm is undeniably more difficult than in a ripple or a wave, but fish can be caught, even in the daytime. And however difficult they are in daylight, there is always a good chance of a fish or two at dusk.

Dry Fly and Drag

When the angler fishes dry fly on a river, he knows that, except perhaps when fishing an artificial sedge fly, he must avoid drag. Even with sedges, drag often puts a trout down, specially in good light; it is at dusk that the large dragging sedge is most effective.

But when the same angler fishes on stillwaters, he seems to find it difficult, if not impossible, to avoid causing his fly to drag. He cannot seem to discard the habit of pulling his fly after casting it out, and even when he does, it is seldom that he takes steps to avoid the drag that is caused by wind or drift acting on his floating line. It is not surprising therefore that the dry fly is little used on stillwater trout fisheries, and discounted altogether by many anglers. Yet the matter of drag is equally important on both still and running water.

On both, the one artificial fly for which drag may not deter and sometimes induces a trout to take, is the sedge; but even that will often attract when no drag is present. On stillwaters, you can pull a floating sedge quite fast across the surface, and at times, trout will chase and grab it. At these times, they will also chase and grab the same dressing that has been attached without any waterproofing and drawn along quite quickly just under the surface, which is a comfort when at dusk you find your dry sedge will no longer float.

Equally often, a dry sedge cast out and simply allowed to sit inert on the surface, until drag due to wind and drift makes it necessary to lift off and re-cast, will catch trout very successfully, and this is a most useful tactic in a flat calm, when the fly can sit for quite a long time without drag commencing. The only trouble is that the take, when it comes, is often sudden and explosive, provoking a violent strike that causes a break. I have even been broken when the rod has been resting on the gunwale or my fishing bag and I have made no attempt to strike; so it is sensible to avoid an over-fine leader point for this method of fishing, specially where there are large rainbow trout.

Among other dry flies that should be cast out and allowed to sit without drag on stillwaters are imitations of both the dun and spinner stage of the mayfly, pond olive, lake olive, and caenis, and

136

among terrestrial flies, the crane-fly, or daddy-long-legs. With all these, and the sedge, it is best to ensure that the entire leader sinks.

I will not pretend that trout will never take a dry fly at the end of a leader of which some part, or even all, is floating; but I am well convinced that the sunk leader catches many, many more fish and that it is well worth taking the trouble to see that it does sink. A little trouble is involved because the proofing agent used for the fly nearly always gets on to the leader to a greater or lesser extent. That is one reason why I avoid aerosol dry-fly sprays; too much goes where it is not wanted.

The stuff for sinking leaders is a very stiff, putty-like paste made by mixing equal parts of washing-up liquid and glycerine and adding enough fuller's earth to produce the right consistency. Drawing the leader through a little ball of this stuff will make it sink directly it alights on the water.

Of all the artificials, the Daddy-long-legs demands the highest standard of avoidance of drag and the closest adherence to correct dressing. It took me many years to realise that when flying or on the water, the legs of this insect are disposed quite differently from when the creature is at rest either on the ground or, as we often see it, on the window. Then the long legs are spread out all round, but in the air or on the water they all trail backwards. I would go so far as to say that the artificial with 'legs' tied so trailing is at least ten times more effective than if the legs are spread out, as is usually done when artificials are tied. The dressing I have found most effective is as follows:

Hook, No 8 long-shank round bend
Abdomen and thorax, brown turkey-tail fibres or dyed swan herl; colour not critical
Wings, a pair of Plymouth Rock cock-hackle points making a V at about 30 degrees to the abdomen, sloping back
Legs, eight pheasant-tail fibres each with two knots tied in it (real flies have six legs but trout can't count and some get broken off in any case)
Hackle, ginger cree cock
Silk, medium brown

The feather fibre used for the abdomen and thorax should be wound over a varnished silk whipping while the varnish is wet, and wound treble at the thorax so as to increase the thickness there.

137

The exception to the rule of never allowing the artificial Daddy to drag is when one is fishing from a boat in a good wave, when it may be bounced from wave to wave, either with conventional tackle or with a blow-line; dapping, in fact. But otherwise, cast it out, don't pull it, let it sit still and only re-cast if drag sets in. If you do pull it, you will often find a trout will follow it as far as you like to continue pulling, encouraging you to repeat the pulling process; but unless the fly goes under the surface, that trout won't take it, and he will seldom do so even if it is submerged. So I repeat, let it sit still.

In passing, I might mention that the Daddy is greatly under-rated as a river fly. It will often catch a rising trout that has ignored the conventional small dry flies, even on the chalk streams, from mid-August onwards. It even catches grayling.

Another dry fly that needs to be let to sit still is the Multiple Caenis, or Lucky Alphonse. This is tied on a No 12 long-shank with three tandem bodies with four cream hackles, one at each end and the other two spaced equally between. The bodies are cream swan herl, the hackles cream or cream badger cock; if cream, the tying silk, which is dark brown, should be exposed at the root of each hackle. It is hard to catch trout when caenis are about but this pattern often gets you one or two – if you let it sit and don't pull it. (Please don't ask me how to pronounce caenis. I say 'see-nis', as in 'Julius Caesar', but I don't know if I'm right.)

To sum it all up, there is much more value in dry flies on still waters than most anglers realise, provided it is understood that as much attention is paid to drag problems as would be required in river fishing. It is by no means rare to find, on these waters, occasions when the correctly fished floater beats the wet fly hands down.

Moving That Fly

For as long as I can remember, I have shared my home with cats. I like cats – and I have learned more from them than you might imagine.

Cats and trout are both predators. In a natural state, they are hunters, living on what other animals they can catch and eat.

So when someone who is comparatively new to trout fishing asks me how flies should be fished, I often suggest that they should go and find a kitten, from about eight weeks to three or four months old, or perhaps a Siamese cat, which is usually willing to behave like a kitten throughout its life.

Tie a ball of wool, or a cloth mouse, to a piece of string and pull it about. See which pulls and tweaks will tempt the kitten or cat to pounce. Notice how, when the ball of wool or whatever it is lies still, the kitten will watch it intently and, when you give a little pull, spring on it. You can learn a lot about how to move a fly to tempt a trout by playing in this way with a kitten.

I don't mean that you will learn all you need to know, because although cats and trout are both predators, there are considerable differences as well as similarities in their behaviour. What I do suggest is that a comparative novice trout-fisherman can build a very sound foundation for building his knowledge upon, by what he can learn from a playful kitten or cat.

If he learns to cast reasonably well, and goes fishing with a modest selection of wet flies and lures, casting out and retrieving with the kitten's behaviour in mind, he is going to catch enough fish to keep him happy until he has learned more about other methods, and about the exceptions to the cat type of behaviour. This is true of all still-water trout-fishing and also of fishing wet flies, nymphs, shrimps and others of a similar nature in rivers.

The late Major Oliver Kite publicised widely what he described as the 'induced take'. This consisted of casting a weighted nymph ahead of a trout, letting the current take it close to the fish, and then drawing on the line to make it move upwards or across in relation to the current. Before it was moved, the nymph was still relative to the current. When it was pulled, the trout reacted instinctively, exactly as the kitten watching the ball of wool lying still will pounce when you pull the string.

I sometimes practise casting on my lawn. If it is a nice day, I am likely to be joined by my friend Sir Bristlewhisker Myers, a middle-aged Siamese cat who lives next door. (We call him Psi for short.) Despite his age he is a very energetic animal, and likes to chase the tuft of wool I have at the end of my leader. He pounces when I tweak it. If I reel in, he lets it go several yards and then does his celebrated 20-yd dash, overtaking his quarry at the last moment. If I lift it up in the air, he springs up after it. That cat behaves like a trout, in so many ways, that I sometimes wonder that he hasn't grown spots. Some cats have – leopards, jaguars, cheetahs and several smaller cats!

139

Sir Bristlewhisker Myers will also take a static bait, but only if he thinks it is eatable, and if it is, he won't thank you to tie it on a string and drag it about on the lawn. I once tried this with a piece of chicken, and he got indignant about it and hissed at me. So remember that there are some kinds of trout food that the trout don't want to see pulled about on a bit of string – or nylon. These include the daddy-long-legs and practically all the ephemerid species, the up-winged flies like mayflies, olives, iron blues, pale wateries and the rest. These flies you have to cast out and let sit still in lakes and reservoirs, or float them down without drag in rivers.

The best advice I can offer here is that if you are fishing a fly that is a good imitation of some insect that trout eat, then fish it in a way that imitates the behaviour of that insect. Most winged insects sit still on the top of the water, but sedge flies do practice take-off runs, so you can pull those quite fast across the surface and catch trout.

Underwater insects can swim, so you can move imitations of those in a cat-tempting way. Trout don't seem to mind if you move your artificial sunk fly or nymph a lot faster than a real one could move. Exaggeration of movement can actually attract them, as can exaggeration of appearance; and in that respect, well, Sir Bristlewhisker would rather chase a cloth mouse than a tuft of wool. He likes it to go faster than a real mouse could. That lets him demonstrate that he is faster than the average feline.

Most predatory animals, and that includes trout and cats, are stimulated by movement. Being a predator means eating living creatures, and living creatures move. So movement is an identifying signal; by and large, if it moves, a predator can eat it. The trick is to move it in a manner that provides the maximum of stimulation. Playing with a kitten will teach you much about that.

Fishing Across the Wind

With few exceptions, trout reservoirs are windswept. Visit them, and you will usually find most of the bank anglers are casting downwind, because it is easier.

But there may be reasons why this is not the best way to fish.

On a big deep water, wind may produce what is called a thermo-cline tilt. This means that the warmer upper layers of water are pushed by the wind towards the downwind shore, and cold, partly deoxygenated water rises against the upwind shore, to take its place. You can often detect this if you wade. You can feel the chill of this cold water striking through your waders. Fish don't care to be in this cold water, so if you feel it, move, even if it means difficult casting.

When trout are feeding on or near the surface, they usually head upwind. They eat various creatures, like midge pupae, pond and lake olive nymphs, sedge pupae, or land insects that are blown onto the water. They move upwind, feeding as they go, till the food gets sparse. Then they race back at a depth of around 6 ft till they reach the downwind end of the area in which the food is plentiful. Up they come again and once more head upwind.

If you cast straight downwind, even if you are fishing in an area where trout are feeding at or near the surface, your fly will be seen by far fewer fish than if you cast and retrieve across the wind. Any naval officer will explain that the classic manoeuvre for avoiding torpedo attacks is to head directly towards, or directly away from, the spot from where the torpedoes are fired.

In trout fishing, you want to do exactly the opposite. You want the torpedo, that is to say, the trout, to score a hit on your fly. So pull it cross the tracks of the trout, not in line with them.

This method has another advantage. When a trout takes a fly fished across the wind, you usually hook him securely in the corner of his mouth. When a trout takes a fly fished straight downwind, there is a good chance that you will pull your fly out of his mouth without hooking him at all. Or you may prick and lose him, and scare him so that he won't come again.

This does not mean that you must always cast across the wind. You have to judge the conditions as you find them. A breeze does not always make cold water rise against the upwind shore. It has to be quite a good breeze, blowing for several hours, to do that. A lighter breeze, or one that has just sprung up, may be blowing land insects off the shore and onto the water at the upwind end of the reservoir. Then you will have to cast downwind if you want to take advantage of what is happening – though you must expect to miss some of the takes.

More often, though, crosswind casting catches more fish for the reasons I have given. It also has advantages in lure-fishing, if you know trout are near the surface. You can let the wind blow your line in a big loop, moving the fly along without your having to do much retrieving. This steady movement is often more attractive to trout than a series of pulls.

Always try to pick a spot where you can cast crosswind with the breeze blowing on the opposite shoulder to the one from which you cast. This helps to prevent your fly from catching in your hat or in your ear.

Carbon-fibre rods help a lot in casting across a stiff breeze, because wind pressure is far less than on thicker glass rods. I have fished with a carbon-fibre rod in a breeze so strong that casting with a glass rod was impossible. It was not easy even with the carbon rod, but I got eight fish in spite of the difficulty on one of these windy days, and I might add that other anglers fishing straight downwind got none.

In a really strong wind, downwind casting actually becomes more difficult than casting across the wind, because it is hard to throw a good back-cast into the teeth of the breeze. There is no way in which a good forward-cast can be made following a bad back-cast.

Fortunately, winds strong enough to affect casting very seriously are not too common, but light winds that destroy your accuracy when fishing too long a leader across the wind are very common indeed. I often read advice about using leaders as long as 15 or even 20 ft. When upwind-moving trout are breaking surface as they feed, and I'm fishing across the wind, I don't want a leader longer than 10 ft at most, and even that needs a lot of thick nylon reaching to at least halfway down the leader. With such a leader, I can cast accurately to individual fish, judging their speed of movement as they approach and placing the fly so that I can draw it across their noses at so short a distance that they cannot fail to see it. And I only use one fly. It is up to me to diagnose what the trout are eating and to tie on a good imitation.

Now, when I talk about crosswind casting, I don't mean that every throw must be exactly at right angles to the wind direction. If I see some fish working upwind, my first throw will probably be at about 45 degrees down and across the wind. If I don't get a take, my next cast will have to be more across the wind, and less downwind. I may end up by casting across and partly upwind, though by then I ought to have put the fly where the trout has seen it. If I've done that several times without a take, time to think about changing the fly.

This way of fishing means that each cast is in a different direction, and with more than one fly, a tangle is certain, sooner or later, especially if the wind is a bit gusty. So I stick to the single fly, and I am sure that I catch more fish in the long run than if I used two or three flies at a time.

Fishing across the wind instead of downwind is just as important when you are out in a boat as it is from the bank. When the conditions are right and the fish are working upwind, near the surface, you can anchor and let the fish come to you, a much better plan than drifting. If you drift out of the feeding area, you have to row or motor back, making a wide detour to avoid putting the fish down, and losing valuable time. You can anchor the boat either across or in line with the wind, and I think the latter is the better plan. If both anglers face downwind, one can see what the other is doing, and crossed back-casts are avoided. Normally, the anglers cast on opposite sides of the boat, but if fish are feeding in a calm lane, it is sometimes better to anchor in the ripple, with both anglers casting into the calm lane from the same side of the boat.

Even when boat fishing, I still prefer to use only one fly!

Constant-speed Retrieve

Many trout fishers have discovered accidentally the value of the constant-speed retrieve. It usually happens when the angler, having decided to change his fly, reels in his line and *bang*! – a fish hits so hard that it hooks itself.

Much the same thing often happens when the fly is allowed to trail behind a moving boat. This is usually called 'trolling', and the rules on most trout reservoirs forbid trolling. (It would be amusing to challenge the rule, because it is easy to prove that the true meaning of the word 'trolling' is the use of a dead fish, leaded and allowed to sink rapidly to the bottom!)

Yet another example of the value of a constant speed of movement of a fly is when one casts crosswind with a floating line, and allows the wind to blow the line into a curve, towing the fly along.

There are, however, other ways of producing a steady movement of a fly, without any pauses, jerks or slowing down. One ingenious method which rose rapidly to popularity in the USA, but which seems now to have gone out of favour, was the 'belly-winder'. This consisted of a large plastic spool, 10–12 in in diameter, strapped to the waist and facing forwards. The spool was very shallow and relatively narrow between plates – rather like an enlarged drum from a Scarborough-type sea reel.

This device was used in conjunction with nylon-backed shooting heads. After casting in the ordinary way, the line was wound round and round the spool with the left hand, which acted on exactly the same principle as the pick-up of a fixed-spool reel. It took a little practice to become expert at it, the secret being to hold the left hand palm up and thumb outwards, letting the line slip through all four fingers.

This produced a very steady retrieve, and had the advantage that on the next cast, the backing shot off the spool exactly as with a fixed-spool reel. Because of the large diameter, the relatively heavy backing, about 25-lb b.s., came off quite smoothly, never having been wound in small coils on a narrow diameter spool. If anyone fancies trying such a device, it would be easy enough to make one from plywood.

Another method of producing a constant-speed retrieve is to effect a perfect co-ordination between rod and left hand. This is done by drawing line with the left hand, starting with the rod point high and lowering it as line is recovered. As the left hand reaches the limit of its movement, the fly is kept moving by raising the rod at the right speed, while the left hand moves up to take a fresh grip on the line, after which the process is repeated. I confess that I have never succeeded in doing this properly, but some anglers succeed with it.

The so-called 'figure-of-eight' method of retrieve can, in skilled hands, produce a fairly steady retrieve, but only at slow speeds, and it is not very satisfactory for nylon-backed shooting heads, being very prone to producing a backing tangle at the next cast. Also, it is rather tricky to perform a left-hand haul in casting, when the left hand is holding a large bunch of line.

Yet another way to bring in a fly at a steady pace, and at good speed, is to tuck the rod under the right arm after casting, with it resting across the right forearm, and then use wrist movements of both hands to pull in line, hand over hand. If the fly is taken, a reasonably effective strike can be made by bringing the right forearm sharply back against the chest, tilting the rod up in the process.

A variation on the crosswind casting technique, which can be used in a flat calm if you find yourself in a deserted area of a reservoir, is to make a cast, then walk or wade a few steps parallel to the bank. This drags your fly along at a steady speed, for as far as you walk, and you can use it with either a sunk or a floating line. The opportunity to do it is rare on popular reservoirs, but it is usually very effective when you can use it. You can walk or wade either backwards or forwards, and as far as you like as circumstances allow, and it can be especially effective if you are fishing from a dam.

I don't mean to suggest that a constant-speed retrieve is always best; on the contrary, some patterns do better with a jerky retrieve, others with slow pulls and pauses. The steady speed seems to do best with lures of various sorts; flies like large Sweeney Todds, Black lures, Missionaries, Mrs Palmer and other big hair-wing or streamer flies.

Early-season Fishing

With the start of a new season, here are a few small points for reservoir trout-fishers to think about.

Early-season fishing conjures up a picture of high winds, big waves, leaden skies, cold water and fish lying deep – so we expect to use fast-sinking heads and things such as tandem lures, Jersey Herds and Polystickles at the business end. Often enough, this is successful. But don't forget the exceptions – which are not all that exceptional.

Black buzzers, alias duckflies, often hatch in large numbers early in April, and there's a good chance of finding hatches of these insects at any time during the season. Last year there were great numbers coming off the water at Grafham during the last week in April, when there was the usual press day. (The authorities invite representatives of the fishing press to a pre-opening day session, and a very good idea it is.)

Trout were rising freely to the duckflies on that day, taking them as they sat on the surface. I'd caught some from my garden pond a week before and tied some imitations to float. They accounted for as many trout as I cared to catch; lures and other large flies did nothing, and unusually, the little floater did better than shallow-sunk pupa imitations.

When the conditions are right for deep fishing with sinking lines and biggish flies, here's a point to consider. Don't retrieve too close.

145

Very often, perhaps more often than we know, trout follow a fly in. Now you can calculate how close a trout must come to an angler before it sees him. It depends on how high the angler's head is above the surface, and to a lesser extent on how deep the fish is swimming, but it is in the region of 18–25 ft. So it pays to get your fly out of the water before it comes nearer than 25 ft. Otherwise a following fish will see you. That swirl you so often see in the very last stages of a close-to retrieve is not, as you may think, caused by a trout dashing at your fly at the last minute. It is made by a trout turning to dash away, after seeing you and taking fright!

So get the fly out before the trout comes too near. With a sunk line, you have to roll-cast to get the line out of the water. Don't roll-cast onto the surface and then snatch the line off again into a back-cast. That causes horrible disturbance, right over the head of that following trout, which is wandering around wondering where the fly he was following has gone.

Roll the line into the air. It's quite easy. Before it can fall, take it into a back-cast. Now your forward throw puts the flyline well out. With a shooting head, only monofil falls over the trout, and lightly at that.

On the subsequent retrieve, there's a fair chance that your trout, now moving slowly out from the bank, will see your fly coming in again. If he hits it, you can't fail to hook him.

A great deal of following of lures and streamer flies is done by trout, and that makes possible a rather amusing sort of teamwork, from the bank or an anchored boat. One angler casts as far as he can and retrieves a big fly quite quickly, while another in the same boat, or very close by from the bank, fishes a smaller fly much slower and at a lesser casting distance. Often a trout that has followed the big fly in takes the other angler's smaller one. Let me make this clear: some take the big one, and both anglers are likely to catch fish. My friends and I have used this tactic very successfully at times, when the conditions were suitable.

The principle is similar to that sometimes used in pike- or perch-fishing, where you can cast far and wide with a spoon and attract fish to a live bait on float tackle that has been cast out to a modest distance.

Now here's something to try on trout that are attacking shoals of small fish in shallow water. We all know how exasperating that can often be – huge fish wallowing about, chomping fry or sticklebacks by the dozen and ignoring all our offerings.

Tie a No 6 Rasputin on the end of a leader about 1 ft longer than the depth of the water. Let that, in turn, be attached to a high-density sinking line. Cast, from 25–30 yd range, into the area where all the kerfuffle is going on, and let the line sink right to the bottom. The Rasputin will float. Let it lie, until you see bow-waves, swirls, or what-have-you fairly near it. Then tweak the line enough to make it dive an inch or two. After the tweak, it will resurface. Tweak it again, and so on till it is time to re-cast. There is a good chance that it will be chomped before then, though. Sometimes, startlingly and without warning, it'll be chomped as it lies still, before you even begin tweaking.

For deep-water work you can also use the Rasputin on a very short leader to fish close to the bottom; it is buoyant, so it doesn't get caught up too often.

I'm sure that it pays to study insects on a reservoir, every bit as much as it does to do so in river fishing. Last year I found a kind of midge pupa that I'd not noticed before, and an imitation of it caught me some nice fish. The freshly caught wet pupa had an abdomen of pale olive-buff with gold bands round it. Yes, gold, really metallic-looking. So I tied a No 12 imitation, with the usual white feather-fibre tufts at head and tail, with an abdomen of pale olive, more buff than greenish, floss, ribbed with narrow flat gold tinsel, and a fat thorax of darker brown-olive-dyed swan herl. So there's another good 'un for your repertoire. You fish it like any other chironomid pupa.

After a lot of experimenting, I've standardised my tandem lure-tying. I use two No 8 long-shank hooks, the rear one up-eyed, the front one down-eyed, and I join them with a strand consisting of three pieces of 12 lb monofil, plaited together. With firm binding and a good adhesive, this doesn't slip; it has just the right degree of flexibility.

Never use wire of any kind to join the hooks of tandem lures. Never!

I still tie these things with big cock-hackle wings, because they look so nice, but for practical fishing I am sure hair is much better. Goat, squirrel and polar bear or (more likely nowadays) polar bear substitute are all good. I don't like bucktail – it's too stiff. For white or pale-coloured tandems, I like to tie in a strip of speckled mallard or turkey over the hair-wing; it gives a more definite outline and the speckling suggests the scaly back of a little fish. A very nice fishlike dressing is as follows:

Body, white wool, ribbed silver thread
Wing, white goat or polar-bear hair
Over-wing, a strip of speckled turkey
Throat hackle, hot orange or crimson
Head, black with jungle-cock eye, or substitute
Hook, tandem No 8 long-shank.

To make it more like a perch, add a wisp of bright blue hackle in front of the orange throat, and wind an orange hackle at the rear of the back body to imitate a tail. You can then call it a Hanningfield Lure.

What to do with retrieved nylon backing used to be a problem. Now I use a waist-attached line container made by Efgeeco. It has a mesh bottom, to equalise air pressure in a wind. The trick is to drop a yard or so of line outside the container before you start to retrieve, catching the line between the container and your belt. That lets you get the rod up without pulling line from under the pile. This container beats line rafts hollow. Waves don't wash your line off it, wind doesn't blow it off, and you can use it anywhere, not just when you're wading.

The more I fish reservoirs, the less I wade, and it makes me laugh to see, as I often do, anglers wading in places where the bank is so steep that they can only get out a couple of yards. It wouldn't worry me much if wading were banned altogether; in fact I think we'd all catch more fish. The only advantage of wading is that it makes you lighter by the weight of water your legs displace, so that you can stand longer without tiring.

Isn't it odd that there are no good anchors provided for reservoir boats? You'd think that for £7 a day at Grafham, £8 a day at Blagdon and £10 a day at Chew [prices for 1996 were £13 for an 8 fish ticket at Grafham], they'd have a decent anchor in each boat, but no. It'll pay you to bring your own, and for waters where you can get your car near the boathouse, you can make one by filling a plastic bucket with wet concrete and pushing in an eyebolt before it sets. Attach it to nylon or Courlene cord – plastic-covered clothes line rots in no time. More often than not, you can catch more fish from an anchored boat than from a drifting one, especially when you know just where to anchor.

One final thing. Casting and retrieving makes your hands wet. With that and the effects of wind, a day's fishing early in the trout season can make your hands sore and cracked. Lanolin hand cream rubbed well in before you start fishing will prevent this.

TACTICS

Hook-hold Failures

The Field's contributors on the subject of angling share an almost uncanny ability to make their readers think. One example was an article by John Marchington, in which the desirability of dealing firmly with a hooked fish was discussed.

Every experienced fly-fisher is all too familiar with the fish that manages to rid itself of the hook. It can happen at any time between when the fly is taken and when the fish is being drawn over the net. All sorts of explanations have been offered for how this can happen. Perhaps the hook point impinges on a hard part of the mouth of the fish, as John Marchington suggests. Perhaps the hook-hold consists of a minute piece of skin.

One unusual case I experienced was that of a trout, duly landed, whose teeth had become entangled in the rough wool body of the fly I was using; the hook had taken no hold whatever. In another case, a fly tied on a large long-shank hook had a half-hitch thrown round the middle of its body: a sort of wind-knot with the nylon round the fly instead of round itself. This fly had jammed hard in the mouth of a fish of modest size, keeping the mouth fully open. The fish was landed.

No doubt there are many ways in which an apparently well-hooked fish can come adrift; but I have come to believe that by far the most common is failure to drive the hook home properly. Except with very small sharp hooks, I doubt if we ever strike a hook in over its barb. What really happens is that after connecting, we keep a tight line and the hook works its way in during the next half-minute or so, in most cases.

Few anglers realise how feeble the strike is. One can find out by holding the end of the leader, handing the rod to a friend, and asking him to strike as he would at a taking fish. Tie a fly to the leader, catch its point in a piece of wet leather, and then see how forcible a strike is needed to cause the hook to penetrate over the barb.

One of the most common difficulties experienced by anglers who, having fished rivers successfully for trout for many years, turn their attentions to stillwaters, is the very frequent loss of fish that seemed to have been well hooked. Such anglers have been accustomed to use small flies, tied on hooks in sizes 14, 16 and 18. It takes a great deal more force to drive home the larger hooks, from size 12 to size 6, that are commonly used nowadays in stillwater trout-fishing.

This is only partly due to the actual size of the hook. There is also the fact that most hooks have unnecessarily large barbs, turned up more than is desirable. Hook points are seldom as sharp as they ought to be, though very few anglers take the trouble to remedy this with a small sharpening stone. There is actually a school of thought that deprecates over-sharpness, on the ground that if a very sharp point comes up against bone, it will bend over instead of penetrating. This is indeed likely with over-tempered, soft hooks, which are far from rare. A correctly tempered hook can be made as sharp as possible, without risk of a turned-over point.

It is now possible to buy hooks that have become known as micro-barbs: much smaller barbs than usual. Such hooks go in more easily, and are easier to remove, but just as difficult for a fish to shake out. With normal, over-barbed hooks, it is worth spending a little time with a fine watchmaker's file or an abrasive stone, in reducing rank barbs.

I am certain that far more fish come adrift through over-sized barbs preventing proper penetration than through under-sized barbs allowing hooks to fall out. More and more anglers, in both trout- and coarse-fishing, are using barbless hooks, and most of them claim to lose no more fish than with barbed hooks. My own view is that there is no need to discard the barb altogether, only to reduce it to sensible proportions.

The choice of hook-shape has some bearing on the matter; the longer the shank is in relation to the gape, the more easily the hook will penetrate, but to a shallower depth, while the leverage tending to wrench the hook free will be increased at some angles of pull. Conversely, a shorter shank in relation to the gape will require more force to pull home, but it will penetrate more deeply and be less prone to levering free. Every hook, therefore, is a compromise in design; and when one examines the mouth of a trout or a salmon, it becomes clear that we must expect either to fail to hook, or to lose after hooking, a proportion of the fish that take our flies, even where the hooks are of the highest possible quality. There are parts of the mouths of these fishes into which it is well-nigh impossible to stick a hook.

We have also to contend with the well-known tendency, at times, of these fish to behave in a way known as 'coming short'. This is really a misnomer, as it implies that the fish stops short of actually taking the fly. In many cases, the fly is actually taken, and with sunk flies, the angler feels a pluck, often quite a violent one. Both salmon and trout have the ability to seize a fly in such a way that they avoid being hooked. No one seems to know how they do this, or why they do it, but that they do do it, there is no doubt.

For centuries, anglers have known this, and numerous ideas have been tried in the hope of hooking a higher proportion. None has been successful. This kind of behaviour is by no means confined to game fish. Pike sometimes carry off a real fish bait, then drop it. Carp and other members of the carp family will pick up baits, run with them, and then drop them, in such a way that the hook is never in a position to be pulled home.

It is curious that this behaviour seems to be infectious; large numbers of fish in a water behave in the same way at the same time. There is no known remedy, except that of waiting until the fish begin to take properly, but it is a frustrating time for all anglers and a very puzzling business for the novice, who is apt to blame his striking, his fly patterns, and the hooks on which his flies are tied.

The point made by John Marchington is sound; more fish are lost by the application of too little pressure after hooking than by too much. A fish hooked by a tiny piece of skin is going to come adrift anyway and it may as well do it sooner than later. If a hook is not fully home, it is much more likely to lose its hold under a light than heavy pressure, which latter will eventually improve the hook-hold.

I am constantly amazed to read accounts of how long fish have taken to land. There are few fish in British freshwaters that should take more than a quarter of an hour to bring to gaff or net, and the vast majority ought to be on the bank in less than half that time.